THE GATHERING
MEETINGS IN HIGHER SPACE

WILLIAM GAMMILL

HAMPTON ROADS
PUBLISHING COMPANY, INC.

Cover design by BrickerGraphics
Cover art by PhotoDisc
For information write:

Hampton Roads Publishing Company, Inc.
1125 Stoney Ridge Road
Charlottesville, VA 22902

Or call: 434-296-2772
Fax: 434-296-5096
e-mail: hrpc@hrpub.com
www.hrpub.com

If you are unable to order this book from your local
bookseller, you may order directly from the publisher.
Call 1-800-766-8009, toll-free.

Library of Congress Catalog Card Number: 00-111728
ISBN 1-57174-206-9
10 9 8 7 6 5 4 3 2
Printed on acid-free paper in Canada

THE GATHERING

Also by William Gammill:
Prune
With Reason, Without Rhyme
The Perfect Poem

In memory of

Audle Allison

*But for him I would not have written this book
and you would not be reading it.*

and for

Samantha (Ms. Dawg)

*One night in April of 1996, she promised she
would stay until this book was finished, and did
just that. Friend and companion for fifteen years,
she was perhaps the only being I have met on the
path who never doubted who she was.*

*From her I learned what it means to love
unconditionally and to serve without expectation.
Thank you for sharing your gift of wisdom and
your generosity of spirit. Thank you for letting me
be your 'thumbs' when you needed them.*

You will be missed.

ACKNOWLEDGMENTS

No book is ever written by one person alone. And I refuse to take full blame for this one. The knowledge and generosity of many have gone into it. But for the wisdom, love, and support I have received from my friends and extended spiritual family, this book would never have been written.

For Mike Rush, friend and editor for twenty years whose support and ability to let me know if my words have said what I meant for them to say, my heart-felt gratitude. Finally, to Laura, Peach, and Lenora, three incarnate angels who have made my life and this book possible, thanks.

TABLE OF CONTENTS

"Anyone who is not shocked by the quantum theory, doesn't understand it."
—Neils Bohr

Preface

The following is distilled from over three hundred pages of raw material, most of it written and recorded during a period of fifteen days in the spring of 1996. Although it begins with an encounter that can only be characterized as "alien," the theme is not alien contact. The theme is human consciousness and transformation. It details a number of events: dreams, visions, visitations, call them what you will. Any attempt to classify or categorize them would only impose demarcations that do not strictly exist—personal experiences that have left me stunned, awestruck, baffled on occasions, ecstatic on others, profoundly affected; but, above all, convinced of their reality. I *know* what I saw. I *know* what I experienced.

While the events detailed here are personal in nature, some may have *im*personal implications; by that I mean they may conform to mystical, religious, or even strictly Christian archetypes. I am not concerned with the language of their imagery, nor am I too concerned with their meanings. I *am* concerned with their accuracy, and I have come to believe that visions are not the prerogative of poets, just as mystical experiences are not confined to saints; nor are encounters with aliens the preserve of lunatics.

Parts of this book will work like a spaceship for some of you, a vehicle into other dimensions, a subtle experience in which one senses a felt relief, or a felt shift. Some of these "encounters" may prove to have spiritual or even scientific significance; they may not. It may be that their sole purpose is to subvert the rational world view by keeping mystery alive. If so, that's enough. But let it be understood: These events, waking or sleeping, are not subjective. That is, my conscious mind does not create them. They do not belong to me in any conventional sense; they happen to me. Always, I seem not to be *having* an encounter, but *seeing* one in which I am involved.

The second half of this book both informs and is informed by that initial experience. While integrating all manner of new information, I am made to witness the destruction of whatever belief system I might have had previously.

Transformation has been described as an *awakening*, a new quality of attention. If so, this book is a conspiracy of transformation—not to impose it on those who are neither ripe nor interested, but to send a signal to those who are. Should you find these accounts difficult or even impossible to believe, then this book is probably not for you; put it aside.

At some point in our lives, it seems, we decide just how conscious we want to be. We establish a threshold of awareness. We choose how stark a truth we are willing to entertain, and how open we are to examining contradictions in our lives and beliefs. Our brains then censor what we see and hear, filtering reality to suit our level of courage. According to Marilyn Ferguson, writing in *The Aquarian Conspiracy,* at every crossroads in our life we make the choice for greater or lesser awareness: transformation is not a spectator sport.

My efforts here are not to convince or convert anyone. If you are not already a believer, this book will not change your mind. My aim is merely to add one more voice to the growing numbers who have been dragged to the edge of reality by something they have seen or experienced; something so totally strange and anomalous that it triggers personal transformation while inducing a kind of religious awe, but something which you cannot, or dare not, confide to another.

Transformation is difficult and singular. It is a journey with no boundaries, no rules, and no final destination. All this is just to say that while it is a lonely path, you are not alone on it.

THE GATHERING

It was during a three-hour period on the evening of April 23, 1996, that most of this material was processed—"channeled," for want of a word—though the experience felt less like channeling than it did a complete inhabitation. I'm new at this so I'm not at all sure what channeling is supposed to feel like. There was no loss of consciousness, no voice change, or foreign accent. More than a dream, more real than any out-of-body experience I can recall, it continued to rattle and revisit my entire person for the next fifteen days. More than that, it triggered a response in me that continues to this day.

I have taken the liberty of editing out some repetition, and rearranging the material in a format personal to me. There will be times when the voice you are hearing will clearly be mine; at other times the distinction will not be so clear. But aside from that, I share it with you as it was presented to me.

I live alone in a small apartment complex wrapped around an open courtyard and situated on the edge of the city. Sitting back from the road,

1

the complex is quiet, if not secluded. I've been living here for several months, working on a book, recovering from a nagging illness. Broke, physically spent, and emotionally exhausted, my life was rapidly approaching critical mass.

I've meditated for most of my adult life, but I'm not one who "prays" in any traditional sense. I have no opinions about it; it's just not something I'm inclined to do. However, on the evening of April 23—an evening noticeably warmer than the ones preceding it—I was walking across the courtyard, near to tears, whining at the stars, shouting at God . . . begging, *beseeching* the Divine Mother to just give me some relief. Take me to the next whatever-there-is; I don't want to understand one more thing. I don't need to process or prepare myself in one more way. Just *take* me.

Back in my apartment, I kicked off my shoes and stretched out on the bed. I had not slept well for days, but suddenly I felt relaxed and soon fell dead asleep.

In the middle of the night—I don't know the exact time—something, a noise or movement in the room, caused me to wake up suddenly. The room was electrically charged; every hair on my body was standing on end. Outside my door a large number of people seemed to be whispering and stirring around. I sat up, put on my shoes, and went out into the courtyard. But it was not the simple tree-lined courtyard I am used to. It had become a huge and meandering rock garden made of small stones in spiraling patterns and pools filled with water. *You* are beside me. I'm not sure who *You* is, but together we are looking up into the night sky, trying to locate the Pleiades, the Seven

Sisters. The sky is clear, the stars unusually bright. Heat lightning flickers in the distance. The air smells like it might after a spring rain. We are not alone. There are hundreds, maybe thousands of people in the garden looking at the stars. There is a sense of pleasant anticipation about everyone, a quiet excitement. No one is talking. It's as though everything that *can* be said *has* been said. When the stars fade behind what looks like a thin vapor of clouds, I think nothing of it. However, they continue to fade until they appear to be behind tinted glass; like looking at the stars through a moonroof. Then, even as we watch, the stars, in a flash of orange light, disappear altogether and are replaced by lights of precise geometric shapes; some perfectly round, some long and rectangular, a *fleet* of lights. I am watching this. We are watching this together as the fleet of lights descends slowly above us all, materializing gradually into a colossal airship, replacing the night sky in all directions.

Even as it occurs to me that the phenomenon we are witnessing is a spacecraft descending on us, I realize that we have been joined by a hundred or more tall beings, very tall, looking like cylinders of light, post holes of light. You know how a post hole is filled with dark before it's filled with post? Well, these were the opposite of that; these were post holes filled with light. And density. Bone-hard post holes of light were circulating through the crowd.

One of them gripped my arm and when I turned to look he had taken on a human form, wearing levis and a blue flannel shirt. He let go of my arm and turned instantly back into light. Throughout his body ran a radiant, electrical fire

3

which seemed to emanate from the heart. Then he gripped my arm again and returned to human form. He did this three or four times, blinking on and off, watching my reaction. For a nanosecond there was a nanosmile. Then he took me by the arm and we were, in the space of a thought, teleported on board this giant spacecraft and into what appeared to be a huge and plush hotel lobby—rich divans, carved tables, silk and satin draperies. It was like the lobby of some Grand Hilton Hotel in the sky, only more so, and bigger than you can imagine; the ceiling must have been seventy stories high.

And the lobby went on forever, in all directions, filled with thousands of familiars: old friends, new friends, some people I'd never seen before but felt a kinship with. Everyone with smile enough to make you wonder what they might be up to if you weren't up to the same thing yourself. Everyone knows what everyone knows; each with the ability to listen to the others' thoughts, communicate with each other, have individual thoughts, and do all this simultaneously.

Some of us, but not all, had these light beings attached to our arms. They each radiated a sort of warmth and friendliness that evoked complete trust. And their intentions seemed totally in keeping with the well-being of the human beings with whom they were associated. The blue flannel shirt-*thing* leaned into my face and spoke to me. Not in so many words did he speak, but in ways that I understood. He said, this is *the gathering*. Do you understand that? And of course I didn't. I had no clues and no notions. He repeated it: this is the gathering, and you have an opportunity to go across on the first wave.

I began to understand that we were all gathering to go someplace—a new port, a new planet, another dimension or plane of consciousness, somewhere—and I was to be in the first wave to go wherever it was we were all going.

I could go, it seemed, with but one condition: I had to go alone. When he said that, I felt like someone had just stuck an ice pick in my heart. The only painful moment of this entire experience was when I realized that I had to be willing to leave everything and everyone behind; my wife, my daughter, my dog, and *You* all immediately came to mind. (Being alone would eventually be more comprehensive than I could ever have imagined. But in that moment, all I could think was that I've come too far not to do the next thing, whatever that is.)

The blue flannel shirt-*thing* seemed to understand that I was having doubts about the reality of everything. He made me thump the table, squeeze the cushions, caused me to feel the deep pain of personal loss, then its relief. This was not a dream, but a real feeling in my body, and he wanted me to know that.

He handed me what appeared to be an eight-by-ten-inch picture with a two-inch frame around it. The frame had a number of hieroglyphic symbols and geometric shapes carved into it. Before I could look closely at any one of them, I looked into the picture and suddenly it became a window into the life I'd just left behind. I could see my room, someone sleeping, I think. Nothing was really clear.

My life in the window looked like a dream or a shadow of the one I was experiencing on board ship. And each time I looked away from the window I forgot every detail of *this* life. I looked back into the window and there it was again, complete with time and memory and stuff going on. I looked away and could recall nothing. The only constant and real thing was my continuing onboard experience, a feeling that persists to this day.

The flannel shirt-*thing* led me through the lobby by the arm; his touch was cool, firm, and accurate. He talked with other light beings; they appeared to make jokes, communicating by thought forms rather than words, all of them dressed in clothes and bodies appropriately like "us." At one point, mine paused to touch one of our group on the shoulder, a gentle tap of acknowledgment that caused a slight electrical charge to spark between the two of them. A lot of other light beings were doing the same thing, generally touching and congratulating this same one of us, whom I judged to be a particularly wise, or courageous, or exemplary one of us—a leader, of sorts. He seemed genuinely humbled by it all . . . innocent.

At some point I was given a visual symbol to hold in my mind's eye, and a personal mantra—a private sound all my own. Together they work like a library card, I was told, a pass into some sort of living library of the universe.

I was led deeper into the ship and delivered through a set of high double doors. Once inside, the flannel shirt-*thing* let go of my arm and immediately turned back into light, then disappeared altogether.

I was alone in the back of a hexagonal gallery filled with hundreds of childlike beings, happy to see me, happy to be there, just happy; all waiting for someone to appear in the center, on stage, and do something.

I didn't have a clue. I didn't know what was going on, what was expected of me, or how to think about it. But I was not concerned. In fact, I felt amazingly free of concern, opinion, or judgment.

Then an old and very dear teacher of mine suddenly appeared out of nowhere and stood beside me. I was surprised. He died ten years ago and I haven't seen much of him since. He tapped me lightly on the forehead and asked if I was ready. "Are you ready to have a go at me?" he asked. The tap on my forehead had the effect of being shot through the head with a pencil. And before I could recover, my teacher and I were on stage together.

I was still clueless, still at a loss for what I was supposed to know, or do, or say. I didn't feel adequate to have a go at him; I felt the moment might better be served if he had a go at me. I told him that. I don't know what I said, exactly, but the entire gallery roared their approval. They were having a good time. They liked me. I had somehow said the right thing.

During my teacher's lifetime, we studied together for twelve years, and, occasionally, our very different personalities clashed. Here, in this moment, as though to put aside those differences, my teacher took off his personalities. In less time than it takes to strike a match, at least sixteen of his faces passed in sequence into my forehead and out of mind, each face looking less like the teacher I was familiar with. Somewhere, around the fourth or fifth face, he began to look very Oriental; and somewhere else, deep behind all the faces of my teacher, was something I can only describe as being his *purposeful intent.* All I saw was a body of light.

Someone handed me a roll of papers, laminated and stuffed into a tube. Each page was covered with maps, drawings, diagrams, formulas, symbols, and words. I didn't understand a single mark on any page. My teacher asked me a question and I realized that this was to be a review of sorts, and it had begun. I had no idea what the first question was, what it meant, or how to answer it. Empty, mindless, I remember thinking how much my head looked like a clear glass bucket with nothing in it. I thought, this is a test and I am in the wrong class. They think I'm someone else. My God, they think I'm *You.*

I don't know what my teacher asked me, but I watched my empty head fill up with information and give him the response he seemed to want. My head emptied and he asked me another question. Again my head filled up with answers and information. And so on. Each time he asked a question my head filled up with answers. Between questions my head was marvelously empty. The crowd of childlike beings began to cheer. I began to cry. My teacher was smiling. A feeling came over me—my heart first, then my head, then my entire body. I thought I was coming. I wondered, is it possible to come forever?

(All this in the time it takes for a bolt of lightning to pass through your skull, your brain, and out again. All I saw was a body of light.)

Now this part of the experience would seem to end right here. I mean, it doesn't really have an ending. What appears to be an ending is but an invitation to access a more vast and subtle scale of operations. I woke up at first light, back in my room, in my bed, feeling like I'd had sex all night with the Beloved. Light and loose in my body, I felt wonderfully hungover from whatever had gone on the night before; indeed, was still going on. I do not remember the stages of my return—at some point I seemed to be more here than there. I looked around and *You* was gone. *You* had decided to stay onboard, I guess. Without *You*, I got up, dressed, made breakfast, and forgot to eat; took the dog for a walk, got lost, and had to be led home.

You know how it is with some dreams that you experience very deeply and when you wake up you want to remember them but can't; you can't recall a single clear detail? Well, this was the exact opposite of that. This was as real, available to the five senses, and as dimensionally realized as anything I'd ever experienced in my normal waking state. I seemed to be living simultaneously in two dimensions of reality, maybe more. Maybe a *lot* more.

I thought perhaps if I meditated, that might help to ground me. But as soon as I went "inside," I had this sensation of astonished flight, the breath of my body became visible, and these living post holes of light were suddenly everywhere. I was right back onboard, surrounded by the gathering.

—from the Journal entry, April 24, 1996

In the Days and Weeks That Followed

In the days and weeks that followed, I walked around feeling stunned and "onboard" most of the time. A casual thought, such as, "I wonder what's going on up there," would result in my being "up there" before I consciously completed the thought. And there were long hours in which I felt like my entire mind and body were being sweetly bathed and drawn through a protracted orgasm. I couldn't make a fist for a week.

And all I had to do was refer to the library card by recalling the symbol and the sound, and my head would immediately fill up with information about things I had not previously been curious about. Of course, it would also fill up with things about which I am curious.

For instance, now that I had something like my ordinary mind back, I wanted to know *who* and *what* and *how*. And, in their manner, they told me.

Most of what was going on was in some way related to the Cosmic Brotherhood, the *Brothers*, emanations from the Creator. In our present expression we are from the star system of Sirius, they said, working with like beings from the Pleiades, using Sirian technology. We are the male aspect of the alliance; the Pleiadians are the feminine. They, the Pleiadians, are the heart of what is going on—the *divine* heart. It is their job to start all this by pulsating the divine heart. The Sirians then hold it in form by use of geometric light, they said. And all of it is being watched over and assisted by the Brothers.

That's what they told me.

A long pause followed during which I can't be sure if they were monitoring my thoughts or waiting for me to collect them. I felt like my hair was on fire; my ears, I'm sure, looked like burnt bacon. That they could hear my thoughts is certain, for they commented on some and ignored others. They told me that their collective purpose on this planet at this time is to accelerate the evolution of life and consciousness as focused through the human species. Our entire planet, it seems, is being birthed into the metaphorical Age of Light. The human race is about to join a universe larger and richer than our wildest imaginings. This is the quickening, the ascension, the rapture, a coming of sorts.

But they cautioned me that the words and labels are mine, defined by my own limitations; that, while they actually inhabit a universe of non-form parallel to ours, they are simply reflections of our deeper selves, our own *divine intent*. In a place, in a way that we are not yet able to comprehend, they are us, me, reflections of our unity before and after matter. As midwife to our birth into form, their job is to enter our consciousness and wake us up.

As for the spacecraft—the Lightship, they called it—where does it come from?

Actually there are two kinds of crafts often referred to as UFOs, they told me. Those on this side, this dimension, which appear to be metallic and can be photographed, are simply mechanical reproductions of what are, in fact, living entities from another dimension. My own experience with the Lightship is of this latter kind. As an actual living being, this type of UFO is organic in nature and increases or decreases in size as you come on board or leave; your own consciousness becoming a part of its consciousness. It does not come from a *place* so much as a *need*, and was originally formed close to the point where matter emerges. It is not really a craft, but a live being, the energy package of the being itself, appearing as something I could relate to—a Hilton Hotel in the sky, or light beings made to look human. What makes it unbelievable and, therefore, unrecognizable, is its enormous size. We don't recognize singular living entities the size of a house, or a spacecraft, or a city, or a whole planet. We are seeing live beings, not UFOs; instead of ships, we are engaging the actual soul of the thing itself. And, as such, it has one of two natures: put simply, it is enlightened or it is not.

I was told not to fear the latter, for we have power over them. They are leaving anyway. They will not be able to stay much longer because of the dimensional shift taking place, the ascension of consciousness, which requires a perfect balance of heart and mind.

With this shift, humanity is moving from an emotional polarization to a greater alignment with higher/clarified mind. The Ascension is an evolutionary process by which a physical Being may extend himself up into the higher dimensions while maintaining the physical body. You don't die at all; you consciously move from one world to another, taking your body with you. True, the substance of the physical is somewhat changed; the physical looks the same, but there is not the density of matter that is experienced within the third dimension. To ascend does not necessarily mean that one goes directly to the *source*, the *pool*, back to the home of the *Creator*, but ascends into the higher dimensions to experience other realities while carrying with him the remembrance of the present lifetime.

That said, there is no three-dimensional model that can accurately explain any of what is going on. For that reason, the Sirians have created a different hologram for planet Earth: a context of reality by which we might better understand some of what is taking place.

For some, this experience will feel like a shift from one dimension to another, lighter and less dense; others will feel like they have been taken "onboard"; still others will simply notice changes in their attitudes and emotional states, enhanced awareness perhaps, or a new sense of empowerment, healing powers, clairvoyance, clairaudience, and so on; some will have periods of lost time, amnesia, even interactions with extraterrestrials; and some will experience a deep rapture, or many small raptures leading up to and away from a larger one. In whatever ways your consciousness can accept it is how you will experience it.

But it will not happen sequentially, or in any way that appears logical. In fact, logic will not help you understand much, if any, of what is going on; reason is your enemy right now. You cannot think your way to the next whatever-there-is. Just know that you have free will and that you agreed to the time and manner of your own awakening. From one level of existence, this is just the evolutionary process in action. You are witnessing, and participating in, an exponential leap from one species to another.

WHO ARE THEY?

Sirius is the brightest star in our galaxy. I just found that out this morning, sitting in the library around the corner from my house. I was thinking about Sirius, about how much I don't know, when it occurred to me that until a few days ago I'd never really heard or thought much about Pleiades or Sirius.

The Brothers, on the other hand, I'd run into before; members of a group mind known as the Great White Brotherhood ("white," as in possessing *all* colors). I was aware of some of their doings, but wasn't really clear about who, what, or where they came from: *emanations from the Creator,* I was told, *thoughts from the mind of God.* I am certainly glad to get that cleared up. (To be more precise, they are thoughts from God responding to our/your own divine intent. We/you intend them; God invents them.)

But the truth is, I know very little about astronomy or stellar populations. And all I know about Sirius is that it is part of a dog-shaped constellation of stars; the dog belonging to Orion, the hunter, and Orion being the result of three gods in a good mood pissing on an ox hide. And that's the extent of my incursion into astronomy.

And it still says very little about Sirius.

So I was sitting in the library reading from a dictionary of astronomy that Sirius is not only the brightest star in our galaxy, but it is also eight-point-six light years away from Earth, and twenty-six times more luminous than our own sun. I was reading that; and while I was reading that, I was being told this, though not in this order: Sirius is the male aspect of an alliance with Pleiades designed to correct a situation initiated in Atlantis thousands of years ago; an experiment gone awry. Along with Venus, Sirius and Pleiades are key players in an experiment being conducted throughout the local universe. Earth is a kind of laboratory, and the experiment has to do with biogenetics and consciousness.

Living man, it seems, is the result of a holographic union between spirit and matter, forerunner to a species that will not even be completed for another thousand years. The entire collective human consciousness will eventually coalesce and become the brain in a single planetary being, its total awareness.

Pleiades and Sirius represent two specific qualities radiating throughout the Universe of Being. The Pleiades represents love and has to do with energy expression. Sirius radiates from truth and has to do with form and structure. To move from one dimension to any other, you must possess these two polarities, love and truth, wisdom and compassion, in a perfect balance.

(The Chinese have one word, *hsin*, which means both heart and mind, of one essence; when balanced and working properly, they are the same thing.)

At the local level in this present moment, the goal is to activate the divine heart and bring light/Christ consciousness into form. The job of the Pleiadians is to focus energy on the human heart, while the Sirians focus on the geometry of the physical body, the light body. But we can accomplish this balance with no conscious understanding of the process. The right intent and a child's trust is all that is required.

The Sirius star system is the sixth dimension of our world, the universe as we know it. It creates geometrical light constructs out of the physical forms in our world. It is holding the light body of the Earth in form. It is holding our light body in form while our divine heart is being activated. In *The Pleiadian Agenda*, Barbara Hand Clow tells us that the Sirians built the Great Pyramid and the Sphinx some thirteen thousand years ago to hold the stargate open while our entire solar system travels through the photon band into the Age of Light. Since that time they have been dormant, or at least imperceptible to the three-dimensional mind.

Until now. This is a cyclic event, and it is time. The Sirians are holding each of us in form while all of this is taking place.

But it all starts in the heart.

You must keep your heart open and your mind still; the opposite is true of most of you. If your heart is closed for any reason, the universe will not, cannot, nourish you. And any act of resistance on your part, the universe takes as an act of aggression. Learn to discern, but keep an open heart.

You can only be accessed through your feeling nature. It is the job of the Pleiadians to open your human heart so that it might be hollowed out and made deeper, larger, enough to hold the divine heart; at the same time kindling a current that is larger than personal agenda, allowing a life force of divine energy to pass through you without destroying you, and in turn be conveyed to others.

As this is going on, the thymus may feel stressed, the heart may get broken. You will have bodily pains and tinglings, feelings in areas you have not felt before. You will become convinced that you are dying. All necessary to make the quickening, the ascension, a living thing in your body; the opening of a new chakra above your heart, having to do with galactic connections and a higher burden of service and unconditional love. You will feel as wonderful and as terrible as you have ever felt in your life, and you will feel both of these at the *same time*—a perfect balance of the feeling nature.

At the core of any balance of opposites is a quiet place. The more perfect the balance, the more profound the peace emanating from it. Very quietly, almost without notice, it comes over you, the realization that there is nowhere anything like the place you are in right now.

I can't begin to explain how these communications take place. They are, at least in part, neurobiological: my nervous system becomes a sort of vibrating channel of communication; my sense of gravity merges with theirs; our awareness blends. We seem to experience reality as one being. The channeled information is just a by-product of a shared simultaneous-everywhere-matrix of reality.

On one occasion I was meditating in the early hours when I became aware of a small pyramid in the center of my head, its base sitting just above and behind my eyes, its apex at or near the crown, that soft indentation at the top of the head.

At first I heard a high pitched electrical hum, like very delicate machinery—a combination of om and the whir of intellect. Then I became aware that the pyramid was rotating, and it continued to rotate until the apex clicked into place somewhere just above my hairline. Then it stopped and the sound stopped and I became aware of another pyramid off in the distance, pointing in my direction, moving toward me. It appeared to be small and moving slowly at first, but then I realized that was an illusion caused by great distance. Coming from deep in the galaxy, it was actually moving very rapidly, only slightly less than the speed of light as it came directly at me.

In an instant, it interlocked with the pyramid in my head, establishing a grid, like a telephone wire, or wires, connected to pyramids all over the universe. I recognized pyramids on Mars, and Venus, and Sirius, and thousands more on planets I could not identify. I was made to understand that each of these pyramids is a repository of living information, and all of them were built, or *birthed*, by a single civilization, thousands, perhaps millions, of years ago.

Now, if this is the means by which all or any of this information is conveyed, I can't be sure. I've never been cognizant of such an occurrence again; however, the image of my head as a relay station remains to this day.

And whether or not you accept my own premise that the consciousness being shared here is of divine/extraterrestrial origin, or simply shared neurosis, doesn't matter. The question remains: *Who* are they?

I still don't know what to call these Beings, other than "the Brothers." I have heard them called angels, aliens, messengers, extraterrestrials, even exquisite data cells emanating from some universal organism. They seem to change labels, names, genders, and identities, depending on the job or function they are providing at the time; the same being appearing to a Christian as a Christian saint, to an Indian as a Hindu saint, to a Moslem as one of their own, and so on. But they are always the Brothers to me, in whatever form; thoughts from the Creator responding to my own divine intent. And the purpose of different disguises is not to deceive, but merely to make themselves accessible to a particular consciousness.

When not in form, they seem to reside in some collective pool of Being, without thought or separate identity.

Whatever personal identity they may seem to have exists only in the context of their relationship with each of us. When they are no longer needed, they go back into the pool. When the next job or situation comes along, they are impulsed into the degree of form or focus necessary to do that job. Between jobs, between situations, between relationships, they simply float in this pool of fully conscious and undifferentiated Being.

But *who* are they? I still don't know.

"We are you," they said, "in ways that you cannot yet hear or comprehend. We speak to you as if we are separate, because that is the way you think of it. All of you are part of this transfiguration, so when different, multidimensional aspects manifest in you, don't assume that you are 'possessed' or in some way mentally unbalanced. Ultimately, you can only be inhabited by your self. There is nothing that you will meet on any plane or dimension that is not 'you' or your creation. The fact of the matter is, we all come from the same place, and when we are there, we are the same thing. There is only one of us here, and it is *you*."

WHY ARE THEY HERE?

The problem is not whether they exist, or in what sense do they exist, but what purpose do they serve; what is their intent?

They are here to assist in the removal of conceptual and emotional blocks that prevent each of us from knowing the God within; and to bring a new state of awareness into all human beings who are able to respond and are willing. In doing so, you must understand that this experiment here on Earth has never been about being saved from your own creation. It is about becoming responsible, awake, and equal to all that exists in the universe. And this is done by bringing all of your collective selves, every dimension of reality, all that you are and all that you know, into conscious focus. If you could do all that, here, now, who would even *want* to leave? The way to arrive in the new world is to be fully empowered human beings. Surrender to the God within, the deep Self of your own divine intent.

In so doing, a new understanding of self is discovered, one that has very little of ego and selfishness in it. You find multiple selves in multiple dimensions; a newly integrated sense of oneself as an individual, but linked with others as if they are oneself, all leading to a merger with something universal and primary.

On an individual basis, you discover a self that is as curious as a child, and fiercely autonomous. It does not compete, but, rather, seeks self-knowledge—not gain, not control over another, but self-empowerment. And surrender is the key; not quitting, not giving something up, but surrendering *into* a deeper level of understanding, a conscious surrendering of personal will to divine will.

Most of you are as fearful of the deep Self as children are of the dark. Yet once you dare to dive into the heart, you find a world of light in which there is no end to going in, no end to opening, no end to your own heart's wisdom.

But know this: As soon as you commit to knowing the God within, you are first made to look at everything that is *not* the God within: Anything "out there" that may own/have your attention—family, friends, lovers, gurus, personal successes, the God of the bible, *any* bible, any fear you might have—will be measured against your sincere desire to know the God within. This is the ascension, and it starts by shifting your attention from things *ex*ternal to things *in*ternal, a shifting of matter into spirit; in this case, a complete shift of the Earth from a *third*-dimensional reality to a *fifth*-dimensional reality. And it is not just the Earth that is evolving. Everything on, in, around, and above the Earth is ascending as well.

Of course the ascension is not the same for everyone. Some of you may bring your body up to a one-hundred percent light velocity and ascend to, say, the fourth level. Others may do the same thing and ascend to the fifth level, or the sixth, or seventh, the eighth, and so on. It makes no difference who you are, what background you come from, or what belief system you are currently laboring under. If you are vibrationally sympathetic, and feel the spirit moving, you will be changed, more or less.

ILLNESS AND DISEASE

The process of the change will affect you in three stages: conceptually, emotionally, and physically. First, your paradigms, the ways you think about your realities, will come unstuck. As your realities begin to shift and collapse—indeed, the very walls may seem to move—you will feel angry, anxious, and fearful. Finally, you may suffer physical stress, actual pains in the body. The Pleiadians are pulsing your heart and liver, all your organs. The Sirians are working on your glands and your endocrine system. As you rethink your entire cellular structure, you may find it necessary to process disease and illness that are encoded in your genetic pattern.

Don't be alarmed.

Stop thinking of illness as punishment for some wrong you may have done. Quite often, when you ask to "*know* the God within," your first experience along that path is to encounter severe illness; it's the challenge that goes with moving to the next level of awareness. In the healing process you begin to look at illness as a spiritual challenge rather than an affliction of matter. In so doing, according to Caroline Myss, you learn how sensitive the spirit is to matter, not the other way around. Indeed, there comes a time in the evolution of every soul when the chief concern is no longer the survival of the body, but the growth of the spirit, the realization of Self.

Moving out of a matter-based reality into one where spirit comes first, you arrive at a different level of truth. You begin to approach healing from a divine perspective, healing the spirit which, in turn, heals the body; and suddenly you realize that anything is possible, any healing. Shifting from one dimension to another, you step not only into a brand new world, but also into a completely different way of interpreting the one reality. From that point on, almost anything you do strictly for yourself is a waste of spirit.

Some of you may be called on to ride the storm of chaos. You may be the healer that is needed in a particular area, or you may be the one who would grow food or build shelters that may be needed. Some of you may choose to continue on in density and matter for the sole purpose of bringing others out of density and matter. Others may be called on to help the collective masses, processing negativity and illness that is not your own, processing for those whose spirit is not large enough or strong enough to do it for themselves.

And all of this has to do with a cause you elected to serve eons ago, your contract with the Creator, to help in the healing of the planetary masses. You said to the gods, "Use me," and they are; they are using your energy fields, your superconsciousness, your very spirit as a means, perhaps, to evolve the masses, or to absorb negativity that, if allowed to build, could result in calamitous destruction.

You may experience tumors, cancers, chronic fatigue; for certain you will feel exhausted and depressed for days and weeks at a time, causing you to require more sleep and at odd hours. Do not take any of it personally. You are one of the Brothers, yourself. And your deep Self knows this; knows, too, that as part of the human species you are just one cell of an emerging being, a species that will eventually coalesce into a single planetary being; and, in order to achieve a successful dimensional shift, it is necessary that the entire species be made well.

Each individual healing is a healing for the species. So you elected long ago to help in that healing, and that's a large part of what is going on with you now. Be grateful. And don't take any personal inconvenience personally.

Illness and disease are not necessarily aberrations. Sometimes they are designed simply to slow you down a bit, make you pay attention and to work with the tools you have. Otherwise you might evolve too rapidly and just explode out of yourselves, back into the pool. Disease is a thing of "matter," and matter is what you are here to experience, learn about, and record.

The human brain itself is not so much a collecting device as it is a reduction valve, a filter, designed to protect you from an avalanche of cosmic knowing, more information than you could ever break bread over—the universe all at once.

(I suspect that the brains of animals work much the same way. But not the brains of gods. In order to know everything at once, God would have to be brainless. Or could it be that what we call "God," is simply an evolutionary urge toward greater consciousness. In which case, consciousness would not be a product of the brain, but quite the opposite. Consciousness creates the *appearance* of the brain, of matter, space, time, and everything else we interpret as the physical universe.)

Meanwhile, as the universe continues to happen to you at an accelerating pace, your vibrations will become rarefied and refined, moving through manifestations of personality, then soul, and finally into spirit, like water changing from ice to liquid to gas. As your light becomes brighter, the personality will become no more than a tool of expression and cease to represent your identity. You will be shown how to heal yourselves and how to do each new thing as it arises, not before. And the exciting thing is: *There is nothing you need do that you're not already doing.* You don't have to learn anything new or take a course of instruction in any of this. It is encoded in your cells. You will know what and you will remember how.

Your Part in This Whatever-It-Is

As a collective event, the awakening/ascension may not have come to your neighborhood yet; it may be years away. But, individually speaking, this event transcends the limits of time and space and is, in fact, already occurring. The actual transformation is not a linear process. It is not a complicated ritual. No mental gymnastics are required. You are not measured by intelligence or talent. You are measured by your courage and a willingness to change in the face of overwhelming opposition. Only fear can hold you back.

You cannot jump the chasm between the three-dimensional world and the next by keeping a foot in one while you land safely in the other. Stop spending precious time preparing for the shift, envisioning scenarios you could not possibly survive. Stop preparing for change by using old survival methods of the three-dimensional world. If you believe in the need for external help such as storing food and clothing, you will most likely need food and clothing to survive. If you are relying on the star brothers and sisters to take you out of this unbearable reality, forget it; stop waiting for truth or power to come from "out there." First of all, there is no "out there"; not really. Whatever is going on "out there" is simply an external projection of what is going on "in here," inside of you. You cannot separate yourself from the whole. Whether it is inside or outside of you, it is still you. Instead of investing in external means of survival, invest in the eternal/internal; surrender to the God within, your own divine intent. What is in your own heart's wisdom will see you across to the other side.

Ascending to the next level of consciousness requires only that you desire to ascend, and that you be willing to raise your level of vibration to meet the level of transition. After that, only one step, one decision, one event is necessary. And, of course, the right timing; the universe possesses impeccable timing. When it's right, the ascension will occur as easily as the next breath. In that breath you must be prepared to give up every preconceived notion, and follow humbly wherever and to whatever pothole/abyss nature leads.

Moving from one dimensional alignment to another is like surfing. You never know which wave will take you there, but you must be alert, ready, and willing at all times. So train your emotional body and your physical body not to react in fear. Develop a habit of trust, and surrender to the God within. When the right wave breaks, suddenly you'll just know. You'll *see* it, and you'll know.

(To "see," by the way, does not mean that your head fills up with people, scenes, and images in great detail, but that you are in touch with some universal intelligence; suddenly you *know* things in a way that you hadn't before—new things, or old things in a new way. Learn to distinguish between the light of *consciousness* and the light of *essence*. The latter has nothing to do with any sort of visionary experience. Being occupied by an image, any image, is to be occupied by the *contents* of consciousness, not the *essence* of consciousness itself, which is without form, without light, without attribute.)

Suddenly, you know with a certainty that precludes anything you've previously known or understood. You realize that all your fears, all your problems and paranoias are just part of a fiction you have built, defended, and maintained by your own stubborn efforts.

It will take awhile for you to become grounded in your new reality. You are being asked to give up the world you know for a world you don't recognize. At first your ego/personality will feel annihilated, blown apart in all directions. Your body will have to be recalibrated, every cell replaced and reprogrammed. Your chakras will function at a different frequency. Expect to feel differently, to think and express yourself differently. Some of you may not like the sensation. New is not always comfortable. Imbalances may occur. Your chakras are very loose, very fluid right now. Your kundalini may be difficult to manage.

There is a part of you, at the cellular level, that will try to convince you that you are dying, you are losing, failing, doing something wrong, being punished for something.

Don't believe it.

The cells are not used to dissolving into light; they are used to taking you down through the death process. They interpret any radical change as dying. And radical change *is* taking place. Each transformation is a kind of suicide, the killing of aspects of the ego to reveal a more fundamental self.

No incarnate life form has ever transformed from the third to the fifth dimension while living in the physical body. It is a totally new experience in creation—and you're doing it.

THE DREAM WELL

For most of you, the transformation will begin in the dreamstate. Your dreams will become more detailed, more vivid, clear, and coherent in ways they have not been before; people will enter your dreams for the first time. Within the dream, there will be introductions to portions of self not previously available. Dreams offer us wisdom, but we sap their strength by too narrow an interpretation, dragging them into too harsh a light, and harnessing them to the ego in order to strengthen its perspective. No wonder we forget dreams; they resist recollection because they do not wish to be pressed into the ego's service.

So don't get in the way. A new chakra is being built, the *dream well*, filled with corrections in thinking, problem solving, and guidance across dimensions. You might have an experience in which you fall asleep and wake up to a different dimension. Your interpretations won't work. You could feel out-of-sorts perhaps, disoriented. This feeling could go on for days and weeks, depending on your willingness to surrender to the change, and your ability to assimilate this rich new diet of light. The surrender must be total; more than just deciding to agree to change your mind, every cell in your body must change its thinking. You must confront the death instinct in each cell, vanquish the illusion of death in every cell. This is a dimensional shift. Don't leave any part of you behind.

WHAT YOU'LL FEEL AND
WHAT TO DO ABOUT IT

Understand, all of this is in terms of one's own focus of consciousness. No one is going to be lifted or zapped by an outside force; very few of you will actually disappear or "beam up" into a starship. The next dimension is not another place; it is *this* place, the process in each of you.

Still, coming back together into your new self may take some getting used to. Shape-shifting involves a bit of shit-shifting as well. Nausea, diarrhea, all sorts of discomfort and disease. You may feel a fullness of the head or ringing in the ears; adjustments to the inner ear may cause you to be unstable on your feet. You may suffer severe headaches as the sutures of your head literally expand due to the downloading of light into your consciousness. The brain itself is expanding. In order to project a new world, you need an evolved cranial hologram. That's a large part of what this metamorphosis is about. You are being given a new brain with new circuitry, and all of this is exhausting to the nervous system.

So lie low during the days and weeks of your coming together, your centering. In fact, the energy will probably not allow you to do much else. Sleep, dream, meditate. Writing in *The Starseed Transmissions*, Ken Carey tells us not to intentionally restrict our spirit, but to go about our business with a minimum of personal involvement. Do not expect much of yourself; do not hold on to things too tightly; and don't worry if you don't understand everything that is going on. All you really need to know is that it *is* happening, and you are a part of it. Your job right now is simply to attend and be attentive. The time for action will come soon enough, and when it does, you will find fulfillment in simply serving the moment that is put before you.

Between moments you don't have to say anything or do anything. You'll not be called upon to convince or convert anyone. You don't even have to consciously know what is going on. Your *presence* is enough. Just *emanate*.

The single most powerful element at play here is your own divine essence. Emanation makes it possible to express that essence in an extremely pure way. It does not have to be accompanied by thoughts or feelings; actions or words are not necessary. It's just there . . . here.

The emanation of presence is about evoking and strengthening divine attributes in other people. Allowing your presence to be fully here for Spirit to use does nothing more than evoke those particular qualities in the people to whom you are emanating. And you don't need to know or do anything. Intention and openness are key, but no technique is involved. You just have to go to bed at night, knowing who you are. Wake up in the morning, knowing who you are. Go shopping, walking in the mall, talking on the telephone, sitting in a restaurant or a theater; do anything, do nothing, but know who you are. And that "knowing" will vibrate throughout your environment, causing the awareness of individual human cells to accelerate exponentially.

As you draw nearer to the vibrational center of your own being, your rate of vibration increases and that causes the vibration of everything around you to increase. What is mistakenly identified as the process of evolution is simply nature's response to your vibrating Being, your consciousness. This defines your task on this Earth, and its performance requires only that you know who you are between moments, and that you be that.

THE PROBLEM IS CREDIBILITY

The problem, as I'm finding out over the last few weeks, is simple credibility. A lot of people just look at me and say, sure, you were abducted by space aliens. Even my own daughter doesn't know what to do with me. She just listens and nods, then looks away, embarrassed, I guess. Indeed, I have lost some friendships by speaking too openly about these matters. My life would have been simpler had I just kept this to myself, but that isn't the reason it happened. And I have long since decided to trust my own instincts, rather than what much of the world would tell me. I mean, in the mind of my heart I know I am not from this Earth, nor are most of you. But who cares, and who's to believe it?

It all comes down to "alien abduction," and describing that to someone who hasn't experienced it is like describing an orgasm to someone who has never had one. Where do you start?

Let me tell you some of what I was told: Our sun is actually a twin star to Sirius A, and is the eighth star of the Pleiades; that our planet is undergoing a complete makeover of all its systems, the end of science as we know it, the endpoint of materialization; that the advanced DNA life forms on this planet are undergoing an acceleration similar to that which atomic particles are subjected to in atom smashers: As we release karma, the antiparticles and electrons collide, quanta of light are formed, called photons (deeply related to thought), and as photons manifest, our karma is transmuted into information.

The photon band is an other-dimensional band of light emanating from the center of the galaxy, its local function being to amp up our light body, our body of consciousness, by turning our darkness (our negative charge) into fuel and feeding it into the light. Raw energy is the result; *other* consciousness. While not analogous to consciousness, the photon is almost surely a major ingredient in whatever consciousness is.

And how, you ask, do I know all this?

Aliens told me.

It happened. Believe it. Believe all of it. Believe everything you hear, everything you read. Believe your eyes, your ears, your intuitions, the small hairs on the back of your neck. Believe me when I tell you that breathing with plants, shape-shifting with animals, and vibrating with Gaia in the rocks and trees, are all functions of the heart. Believe history, every version of it. Believe the weather, trust the forecast. Believe in God, the afterlife, after*lives*, angels, aliens, unicorns, rain on Thursday. Believe me when I tell you that I am one of them, thrown away. But it doesn't matter.

What does matter is that suddenly I *know* it. All of it. I mean, just as certainly as I know all *this* without knowing how I know it, I know *that* in the same way.

That said, how do I tell my wife that, in a sort of out-of-body dream I had a telepathic sense that the mental breakdown she seems always on the verge of, is not my fault, but is more likely connected to the fact that we are all mutating together, becoming multi-dimensional beings. Some of us are more conscious of this than others, which simply means that we get to experience the pleasures of having more light flow through us at the same time we are suffering the inconvenience of having our old world dissipate before the new one is completely furnished and habitable. How to tell her that, contrary to appearances, the world we thought we knew no longer exists; in fact, hasn't existed since 1972. She can stop anticipating the end of the world. It has already come and gone.

Two different star systems reformed an old alliance in 1972 to keep the polar axis of Earth from flipping due to a great explosion in the Sun. As a result, it only flipped a little bit, and even that was hidden from us by the creation of a holographic protection field around the Earth intended not only to protect us, but to accelerate our own evolution to the point where we can protect ourselves. A lot of people changed their personalities at that time. I suffered a series of seizures and went from being some sort of werewolf to pretty much the way you see me now. My wife changed her personality a little bit, then changed it back, then changed it again, back and forth, back and forth. You get the picture.

But how do I tell her that, not only is it possible, it's *normal* to be several beings in several places at the same time; that her subtle/other bodies have already transmuted and are living full lives in other dimensions? It's only her dense body, this three-dimensional vehicle, that still has old programs and processes to live out. The difficulty lies in not yet being able to fully synchronize the doings of the mind with the doings of the body (or bodies). The result is that we sometimes feel fragmented, fractured, and frustrated. In her case, she insists that I'm nuts and that I'm giving her, if not a nervous breakdown, at least a migraine.

How can I tell her that if she'll just follow the connections between things, she can be anyone, create anything? There is no need to recriminate against yourself. Simply notice what you've been choosing and choose something else. This expanded awareness will harmonize her body to any vibration that she can detect, so let her body— let your body, for that matter—lead in making choices; learn to intuit your way along. And the more you trust this new way of responding to your environment, the happier you, she, we all will be. How can I tell her this?

When she asks, "Where did you read all this; where did you hear it?" How can I tell her it's about this dream I had while eating an apple, having sex, playing with kittens and snakes and toads, decoding the real meanings of words and symbols written on the walls of my study? It's about this dream I had; indeed, am still having. I mean, how can I tell my wife that, without sending her right over the edge? And so what if I do?

A UNIVERSE OF INTENT

The next time the Brothers showed themselves, I thought I was ready for them. How can I know more, I asked. How can I know more, and what do I do with it?

You already know everything, they told me. By your intentions, by your light, and by your breathing, you can know the next thing and what to do with it.

The underlying substance of the universe is *intent*. Your intent, and where you fasten your attention determines your manifest universe. There is but one intelligence, one current running through all creatures, through everything; but, as it is channeled it is focused in many different ways through the *purposeful intent* of the different dimensions and varying situations, like a high voltage current passing through a series of step-down transformers. Intent radiates fields of energy not visible to the physical sight. Your needs—for survival, security, self-esteem, a sense of belonging, your spirituality, even the tragedies of your life— are all part of your intent.

Of course no one intends tragedy in their life, but they do choose to learn the lesson that the tragedy represents. That was your intent. That is why you linked those pieces of consciousness together—to meet some instinct, some need, some desire to learn. Each of you represents a biogravitational thought field drawing matter to you, creating the universe around you as you go. You are not only yourself, you are everything surrounding yourself, the whole context; the being behind all things, the awareness behind and beyond all things. You know this in spirit. To know this in body is to be conscious. To know in body what you know in spirit is what it means to know yourself/Self. And you have the ability to generate the quality of individual self perfect for each occasion.

The universe is malleable and exists entirely in your One Mind. As the power of your intent increases and becomes more acute, the power of your instinct, drive, and desire—whenever and wherever focused—will intensify as well. Be conscious. Be aware. Be clear what you intend.

The universe is always one hundred percent on purpose and by intent. The mystery of the universe is that it is constantly rearranging itself to accommodate your own personal view of it—what you want to see (intend) is what the universe is eager to show you. And it does this for each and every one. It does it without judgment, without opinion. What you want, the universe wants you to have. What's more, when your view changes, the universe changes in order to remain consistent with your particular view at the time.

(It would seem to me that the universe is static; only consciousness moves. For example, in

Isaac Newton's day, the universe was thought to resemble a giant machine—Newtonian mechanics. That doesn't mean that *relativity*, or *quantum*, or even the new theory of *chaos* was not already at work in the universe. It just means that our consciousness had not evolved sufficiently to appreciate or even be aware of their existence. So everything we thought, saw, or did, seemed to prove Newton's view. None of which is to say that Newton's view was wrong; just incomplete.)

Still, I had to ask, how does the universe know what I want?

By watching to see what you are fascinated by, what you find compelling, thrilling, mysterious, horrifying, gripping, dreadful, or awesome. Then, once it knows what your preoccupations are, without any sort of value judgment, the universe gives you exactly that. Be fascinated with what you don't want, and you'll get more of what you don't want. Be fascinated with what you do want, and you'll get more of it.

ONBOARD SURGERY

The next several days were very manic as I vac-
illated between two emotional points of view,
ecstatic on the one hand, because of my new
found *what?*—I still wasn't sure; depressed on the
other, as my life before *what* crept back into focus.
Prior to this whole series of events I'd suffered
through days and weeks of depression brought on,
I'm sure, by my only daughter's wedding two thousand miles away which I was unable to attend.

I was broke, bankrupt in all departments:
physical, mental, emotional; what spirit there was
seemed to be elsewhere. Fifty-something and all I
had to show for it was half of a book and an
enlarged prostate.

Understand, I grew up with a manic sense of
my own self-worth. Somewhere during my adoles-
cence I developed such low self-esteem that when
I was elected king of my senior class I thought it
was done as a joke, an act of ridicule. At the same
time, I secretly harbored the belief that there
was/*is* something special about me, something
singular if not superior. For the most part I am genuinely happy at this time in my life to be penniless
in a room in Oklahoma City writing this book.

For the most part.

However perfect though the universe may be, it is not always convenient. And in my adolescent days, mostly I just felt shat upon.

That's the way I feel today, on the eve of my daughter's wedding; abandoned by God and all. And the feelings surrounding this singular disappointment are what set these next events in motion.

It was late afternoon and I was walking through the park on my way home from somewhere. I don't remember where. It doesn't matter. It was cool, airish, but the sun was bright. I stretched out on a concrete picnic table and immediately fell "inside"; and didn't know it until four of the Brothers had me on board, stretched out on a long white table, and sectioned off into four parts. Each of the Brothers began working on a different part or body of consciousness. They seemed to be reaching into my nervous system and removing dark pockets of ganglia that, in their hands, turned into symbols, images, and equations— things that caused me to feel heavy and heartsick all over; but useable information to them. They were gathering data about the material universe, it seems, and that data was collected and stored in the cells of my body.

You can only be accessed through your feeling nature, they told me; your deepest, rawest feelings cause you to open to new information and ultimately the healing that comes with it. Sometimes, they said, *a heart must be broken to open.*

And even as they said it, I felt my own heart break; indeed, I felt like a thousand hearts were breaking inside me all at once, all of them opening and healing at the same instant. I seemed to oscillate back and forth between moments of lucid and total identification with some universal awareness (oneness?), and brief lapses into familiar patterns of thought and thinking; the hard, day-to-day shit of it.

You are here, they told me, on this planet at this time, simply to perceive matter from the same perspective with which matter perceives herself. Your job is not just to observe the material universe, but to experience it deeply, intimately, and totally. That experience is then recorded in your light body and stored as karma, to be retrieved from time to time as need be, in the building of the New Day—Earth after her ascension.

Of course I wanted to know *whose* need? *whose* karma? and when are we gonna be free of all this?

That's when they told me a peculiar thing. They told me that we, you and I, are not here to avoid or even eradicate karma, but to generate it. While we are in this world as a part of this bio-genetic experiment, we will always create karma. Planet Earth is moving from a three-dimensional reality to a fifth-dimensional reality and there is no map for where we're going because *we are the map*; we are not creating a database, we *are* the database. It is from our karmic experiences that hard information governing the physical universe is gathered by the Brothers. Without that information they have no real sense of what is going on here, or what its like to be in a physical body moving through the material universe. Without us, they don't know.

Every one of our acts is interwoven into this mental structure called karma. As we create and then release karma, quanta of light are formed, and cosmic energy, called photon energy, manifests. As this photonic light increases in our solar system, our karma transmutes into information. The increase of healing/saving information is directly related to the increase in photon energy resulting from the collision of karma with the life force; light is information.

To be karma free does not mean that we will not continue to create karma. We will. That is our job. What it does mean is that our acts will no longer cast shadows. We will be active, and we will continue to participate in this blossoming experiment, but relatively free of its burden; *in* it but not *of* it.

And that's where the Brothers come in. Call them angels, guides, bodhisattvas, whatever. They come to remind us of who we are and what we are, and what, in fact, we are really doing here.

But they are not mind readers, they don't know what we're thinking, or even what our specific needs might be.

Until we tell them.

Until we *ask*.

They are sensitive to our requests, our prayers and pleas for help. Our job will always be to generate and collect karma; their job, to see that we survive and be uplifted by it. But they cannot interfere uninvited.

I watched this bloodless operation with curiosity but without anxiety, without fear. And each time they reached inside me and emptied a cell of its dark information, they replaced that cell with one of luminous gold light that caused me to feel an overall sense of well-being.

On a picnic table in the park, on a cool and sunny afternoon, I came awake suddenly, knowing that all my karmic charge cards had been canceled. Instead of worrying about deep debt, long term credit, and high interest, now I pay as I go; and am, in turn, repaid out of the abundance of Spirit.

— from the Journal, April 24–May 8, 1996

FROM THE POND

Things leveled off for awhile after that initial few weeks. My nervous system settled down. When I went for a physical in June, I was surprised to find that my blood pressure, blood sugar, and prostate were all normal for the first time since I could remember. For twenty years I'd had trouble with my back, caused by a herniated disc, and suddenly that seemed to have corrected itself as well. I was healthier than I'd been in years, and getting healthier every day.

A lot of things changed.

My friends changed. Old friends I'd known for years turned out not to be such good friends. I'd been in such awkward straits for so long that my friends had come to expect it of me. Now that my straits seemed easier to navigate, they thought something was wrong with me. My weirdness and their weirdness were no longer compatible; I had crossed the line. We've all been brought up with such a literal-minded world view that we demand that things have only one identity, one meaning. And when something extraordinary breaks in on us, transforming the mundane into something sacred and amazing, we are just not equipped for it. I lost some friends. I continue to lose friends. But others have come forward, so it all works out.

Strangeness continued to happen to me, though its occasion seemed less dramatic, due, in part, because I came to expect it. At the same time, I began to recollect and revisit similar experiences I'd had throughout my life, going back to a very early age; experiences I'd had but had no language for at the time, and certainly no listening audience. My mother didn't want to hear me talk about Venus, or the Moon, or star people visiting me at night. She didn't want to hear it, so I stopped trying to tell her.

But now, with these recent events, it was like a thin film had been removed from the surface of a pond, exposing what was going on in the waters below. I began to relive what was going on; what had, perhaps, been going on all along.

And the nature of the encounters took a peculiar turn; by that I mean their whole perspective began to open up, taking on new costumes, new props, a different imagery. Indeed, there was more "onboard surgery," but there were other things as well.

One such encounter took place on Independence Day, though I'm not sure what, if anything, the date has to do with it. Spring ran right on through June then stopped suddenly. There were a few days of rain and when the skies cleared it was another season. It was mid-summer—hot, humid; the wind, what there was of it, was full of dust. I woke up feeling like I needed to go somewhere, take a ride, for no other reason than my spirit saying let's get out of town for awhile, see some country. So we did.

East of Oklahoma City, between Jones and Arcadia, is a Kickapoo Indian reservation. A forty-minute drive from downtown, the reservation is a well kept secret, and well hidden, unless you know what you're looking for. I found it by accident a couple of years ago, while I was driving around with no destination and all my sensors open.

The entire reservation is an elbow-shaped stretch of dirt road that runs for less than a mile along the Deep Fork River on one side, deep corn fields on the other. There are perhaps a dozen families; fewer than one hundred inhabitants living in frame houses, tar paper shacks really, sitting so close to the road that it serves as their front yard.

But the marvelous thing, the thing that saves it, and brings you up the first time you see them, are these long thatch huts built behind and away from the houses. Woven by hand and open on the sides, the thatch huts are used for sleeping and living in spring and summer.

I turned down the dirt road, drove past a sign that told me this was a private drive, and parked between a wide mudhole and a field of corn. Intending to go down to the river, I walked along the road, watching the river for a path down the clay embankment, until I came to a field of corn that towered over me. Curious, I stopped and peered into the field, looking for I don't know what. Not sure why, I quit on the river, and stepped between two tall stalks of corn. I went in about ten feet then stopped and looked around. Amazing. I could not see the car. I could not see the road. If I were to close my eyes and spin around, I'm sure I would have been lost. Which is sort of what I did.

On an impulse, I closed my eyes and began to feel my way along, slowly, deliberately, between corn stalks. I did this for several minutes, until I became aware of voices up ahead, and wood smoke. Actually, it was more of a suspicion than an awareness; it was faint and apparently far off. So I was surprised when I opened my eyes and stepped suddenly into a clearing. I was standing at the edge of the corn field in someone's backyard.

There must have been fifty Indians of every sex, size, and age milling around in that backyard, squatting on the ground, sitting on lawn chairs and castoff couches with the stuffing coming out, having, I guess, an Independence Day picnic. Can that be?

No one saw me at first, standing there in a corner of the yard, the corn field at my back, with a look, I'm sure, of pure amazement on my face. I had no idea where I was or how I'd come to be there. My reflex was to step back into the corn field and disappear. But by then I'd already been seen by half the party, and soon the other half was looking too. All movement slowed to a crawl; time came to a stop; no one was saying a word.

There was a woman bent over a skillet, stirring the fire. When she saw me, she stood away from the skillet, wiping her hands on her apron. There were a half dozen small children, a dozen sulking teenagers, their parents and grandparents, a dog or two, and a goat the children seemed determined to milk or ride or both. There was a huge kettle of corn, roasting ears, and a galvanized tub filled with watermelons floating in ice water; behind all that, on the road and in the front yard, were ten or more old cars and trucks. Below one of the tailgates, a

53

woman crouched on her bare haunches, holding a wailing child against her while she peed.

After a long moment in which none of us seemed to know what to do, a big man, heavy and wearing levis and a straw cowboy hat, stood up and came toward me, smiling but tentative. It seemed to take a long time for him to cross the yard, everyone watching me watching him, and hard to tell what was expected of either of us.

I smiled. What else could I do?

I had come upon something marvelous and I did not know what to say or do about it. So I did nothing. I said nothing. I was pleased and amazed. Nothing else seemed necessary.

The big man continued walking toward me, moving between worlds, beginning already to step over the boundaries of what I think is real and present. He was already feeling, hearing, knowing what else is there, a larger life than I am yet aware. He picked up a long hunting knife and stuck it in his belt. Then he bent over the galvanized tub and picked out a watermelon, carrying it toward me in both hands. He too seemed pleased and amazed to find me suddenly standing in his backyard. He smiled, put the melon at my feet, and broke it open in the middle, offering me the juicy, red heart-meat.

I bent down and plunged both hands into the melon. There was a sudden click and a shudder, not of light or sound, but of *something*, and I found myself bent over the body of a young buck deer with my hands thrust deep into its slit belly; a yearling I'd killed and brought home to eat. We were all wearing buckskin. I was an outlaw living among outlaws, all of us because there was no other way. I was hunting, poaching deer to feed several families. One night with my hands inside the belly of a deer, I felt the universe fill with dark blood, a warm ocean in a sea of night, the Milky Way wrapped around the sky in awful tenderness. Life, I thought, is terrible only so long as we cling to belief in a human God, and in that moment, I experienced an order of joy and attunement to something very close to the bone; something like love or justice but larger, and having no name I knew.

I stood up, eating the melon with my hands, getting it all over my face and down my shirt. The big man laughed. I laughed. Everyone laughed. I wiped my hands on my jeans and stepped back. We nodded and smiled at one another. Then I turned and took off back through the corn field. I walked quickly and without caution, retracing my steps until I stumbled out onto the road. By the time I reached the car what had seemed dreamlike, hardened and became actual. Once inside, I put my forehead on the steering wheel and began to cry, my breath coming in sudden jerks, I felt glorified, I felt humbled, I could not stop crying. And when I looked up, everything was gathered in a ring of pure and endless light.

I don't remember driving home but I must have.

I felt wonderfully useless the rest of the day, sleepy, but in a nice way, almost blissful. I napped and read, napped and read. Went to bed early, which, for me, is anytime before midnight. I slept deeply and peacefully for a couple of hours, then woke up about two in the morning electrically charged.

I got out my note pad and began to take dictation.

I don't know what I expected, but it certainly wasn't what I got. The information that came through did little to explain or shed any light on the events of the previous day. In fact, the two seem not to be related. And that is significant, because that's what always seems to happen. The link between the visionary encounter and the information surrounding it is either nonexistent or too subtle for me to apprehend. What does happen, what has become increasingly clear, is that the energy of one stimulates activity in the other. The visionary experience opens a doorway, a vortex, allowing the information to come through. However, the vision is its own self. The information is its own self. Each has its own message. They are not necessarily related.

I had so many questions, and so much was available to me in those hours before dawn that I didn't know what I needed to know first, or most. And I have come to realize that no matter how simple or narrow I think my questions are, their answers, though sometimes embarrassingly simple, are never that narrow. I wanted to know about things like karma and reincarnation. Do angels exist? Where do they come from? What exactly is a hologram? What role does ego play? What role spirit? How does God fit into all this? Who are the "greys?" And what about Christ? I wanted to know more about the who, what, and why of my own situation, as well as the world around me. What's *real* anymore? Where have I come from? Where am I going? Am I winning? If I wanted to pray, what would I pray for? And so on. That's when they told me the following.

Quantum Beings/ Multidimensions and End of Time

You, meaning "we," are not as firmly situated in time as you, meaning "we," assume. And it is your, meaning "our," limited understanding of time that inhibits your, meaning "our," growth as a species. Any theory of linear time and space, they assured me, is an illusion, a convenient fabrication.

In a multidimensional world, past and future are woven in such a way that one does not always and necessarily follow the other. Cause and effect are erratic. Sometimes the first precedes the second, sometimes it's the other way around. Karma becomes an anomaly.

In a multidimensional world every event that you perceive in linear time plays out every possible variation of itself on multiple levels. In other words, all realities occur simultaneously. In linear time you can only perceive one lifetime at a time, one variation of an event. For you, this lifetime, this perceived variation, is the "real" one. But this is not the only lifetime you are experiencing right now. This may be the third density portion of it that responds to our five senses, but it is all happening; everything you are or have been or will be, every incarnation of yourself is happening to your consciousness right now.

You are quantum beings. Your natures are quantum. The human species moving through time is moving through a quantum reality, not a linear one. As a species you are in a constant state of super position, both nowhere and everywhere. All possible variations of how an event *could* unfold, *do* unfold, and are just as real in other dimensions. The difference being in where your consciousness is centered.

The Brothers seem to see time as being to our left and our right, future and past. But when I ask them a question, *any* question speculating on a future or past activity, they respond in a way that is confusing to me. They do not seem to make decisions or predictions or even comments that take them out of the present time. They seem to live totally in the present moment. If it is in the flow of things, it happens; more than that, it seems to already be going on.

I asked what I thought to be a reasonable question: How can I accelerate the awakening?

If you mean, how can you make it happen sooner, they said, you can't. It is in the course of things and it happens in the course of things. Only your perception of its occurrence changes. For some of you the awakening is already taking place.

If by "accelerate" you mean amplify the energy, that's another matter. If it's important for you to amplify the energy and "go forward" in the world, just stick your finger in a light socket, or step *away* from your center. Each time you leave your center things *seem* to accelerate; the further away from your center, the faster they *seem* to go, and time becomes an issue, until somewhere, out around the very edges of your energy field, time takes on the characteristics of a law with fixed value.

Nothing could be further from the truth. Time is an illusion. The awakening is peaceful, instant, everywhere, and *now*. To discover the illusion of time, or to *un*discover time itself, you must go into your own center. All of you have an activity—meditation, visualization, prayer, walking, running, whatever—that brings you to center. Whatever that activity is, discover it, commit to it, and *apply* it. As the awakening happens to you, it is important that you bring yourself to center more and more often. Stay there. Practice staying there. In fact, your own divine nature will find ways to make you miserable if you don't stay centered; causing you to stay "in here," even as you seem to be performing "out there," in what you call reality.

The awakening is a current universal event, but it is not happening "out there"; it is taking place *inside* of you, each of you, in this very moment. The real frontier is the moment that surrounds you now, which is outside of time. The present is always outside of time. In fact, time as you know it is coming to an end. The prophecies are true; this is the "end of time." That doesn't mean that the world is coming to an end; it simply means that you are giving up linear time for holographic time—time measured by events rather than calendars. In a truly malleable universe, time is not a quantity but a quality; it exists, but cannot be measured.

Stay in the moment. Live your life as though it had been created for one special event, an event for which you have already been prepared and given the tools necessary to perform it. What you don't know is what that event is or when it might occur, so your duty is to pay attention to each single moment. That doesn't mean be fearful or anxious, just attentive. There is nothing you can do to elude any moment but cultivate an openness to the unknown so that whatever occurs you can be fully present for it.

Keep your prayers in the moment too. Never pray in supplication but in *gratitude*. To want something is to desire that which you do not have. Praying for something you want pours the condition of that prayer into concrete, so that you always want and will never have the object of your prayer; it actually pushes it away. Instead, be thankful in *advance* for that which you choose to experience in your reality now . . .

They continued to respond to my inquiries, and I wrote straight through until dawn. In fact, over the next several weeks and months they continued to respond in ways that were comprehensive though not always direct, not always understood or even recognized until much later.

Spirit/Ego: The Noble Experiment

Living man is the result of a holographic union between spirit and matter, it seems, forerunner to a species that will not be completed for another thousand years.

The entire collective human consciousness will eventually coalesce and become the brain in a single planetary being, its total awareness. Spirit and ego are two facets of that awareness. Sharing the same body, they are like intertwining threads of DNA—that close, that important to one another.

The body is spirit coalesced into a form that the senses can feel, see, and smell; the mind is spirit in a form that can be heard and understood. Spirit itself, in pure form, is neither of these and can be perceived only by refined intuition. Spirit is a direct experience, but it transcends this world. When you gain knowledge of any single thing in the universe, you gain limited knowledge; when you gain knowledge of spirit, you become knowingness itself.

Accessed through the right brain, spirit is holistic, creative, curious. It is the energy of God within each individual; in spirit we are all fragments of the same Source, the Creator/God. Ego is a reflection of that spirit, different only in function. Like the image in a mirror, there could not be one without the other. Ego is left brained, concerned with practical matters; in the beginning it did little more than remind spirit that its body needed water, food, rest.

The ego was created to watch over and maintain the material plane and the requirements of the body. It has been doing this, successfully, for a long time; in fact, since *linear* time began. Without it, or if the spirit had been left in charge of the body and its stuff, the body might not have survived long enough to inhabit or learn anything. Spirit, being insensitive to fear and caution, would no doubt have damaged or destroyed the body through some careless oversight, something as simple as forgetting that the body was incarnate—unable to fly, jump off tall buildings, or drive on the wrong side of the freeway without dire consequences.

So, the ego's job is to lobby for your physical needs. It is not the enemy. It just has a limited view of what is going on; limited to its own material domain. And it is defensive about what it knows, or thinks, or thinks it knows. Fear is one of the tools it uses to monitor and modify your behavior. Indeed, the physical body of the three-dimensional world has fear built into its DNA structure. As you overcome fear, you actually trigger a change in your own DNA; the new human species will eventually possess a six strand double helix DNA structure instead of the current single strand double helix. The third strand is already being wired up; you are feeling the effects of it even as you read these words. In the meantime, in order for the body to develop and fully integrate into the material world, it was necessary, at least in the early stages of transition, for you to give up all memory of your origin in spirit. Of course, you had no idea how total that loss of memory would be, or what effect it would have on the ego.

Ego, with no memory of anything more than its own material domain, began to think that, instead of overseeing, it actually *owned* everything.

Until now. With the timely reawakening of spirit into the body, ego is being made to surrender what never really belonged to it in the first place. At the full awakening, the birth of the new planetary being, ego and spirit will meld together into one thing, the same thing with different but complementary functions. Until then, each time you expand into a higher level of awareness, assume more spirit, you threaten the ego's comfort zone, and it responds by making you fearful of your own life, thinking to escape from the body. In actuality, the ego is being made to suffer its own death. You will, indeed, feel like you are dying.

What you may fail to recognize is that *the awakening has already taken place.* As spirit, you are already living fully, vitally, and expressively in the *moment* of the awakening right now; an event that does not diminish the ego, but merely washes away the illusions that make ego miserable by releasing it from the bonds of gravity, anger, and fear. In truth, Spirit is never fearful, and certainly isn't in a hurry to escape the very vehicle it has chosen as the means of its expression.

The task at hand is not one of eliminating, but of educating and integrating the ego into that awakened moment. This is done by simulating linear time, and walking the ego through the process of the ascension, step by step, emotion by emotion, one heartfelt feeling after another, walking the ego across from one dimension to the next; in the case of planet Earth, from the third dimension through the fourth into the fifth, the dimension of Christ-consciousness.

And yes, the next dimension will appear to have a physical expression; it just won't be as dense as the one you are leaving. Once you are there, and fully housed, the next dimension will seem pretty much like the previous one, but with fewer limitations and less density. The ego's job will then be to govern the physical expression of the new dimension, the same as it has been doing for the one left behind, but with closer and more *conscious* collaboration with spirit.

Of course the laws manifest differently from dimension to dimension, so the actual performance of ego's job will change somewhat. You are shifting from being linear to holographic, from organizing your time and your lives in a linear fashion to being holographic, parallel, simultaneous. But as long as there is a physical expression at some/any level, there will always be need for an ego to manage it.

So, the ego is presently being asked to perform tasks it is not familiar with, in a dimension foreign to it. How difficult is that?

Like any new job, it is awkward and frustrating at first; it can and will make you angry, fearful that you'll not be equal to the task. That's why there is so much anger and fear and frustration on the planet and in your personal lives right now. It is as though you've been right-handed all of your life, indeed, many lives, and now, overnight, you've been told to become left-handed. At first you wouldn't even be able to write your own name. The ego is going through that. It is like a small child, eager to do what you ask, and frustrated because it doesn't know how.

To make matters worse, because you are an entirely new species being birthed, the ego has no functional model to pattern itself after; no one knows exactly what you are destined to become. There is no map for where you are going because no one has been there yet. You are the map. You are the living prototype. You are not building a database for a new species in a new civilization, you *are* the database. Your hard ego experiences are being registered on your feeling nature and recorded in your lightbody like data being banked into a computer. And every piece of information is important. Every mistake, every correction, everything attempted that does or does not work out, goes into the data bank: you.

And the ego must be taught to navigate through all that without losing its body or its composure.

—from the Journal, July 5-10, 1996

Synchronicity?

Each week I get a massage or a chiropractic treatment. After that treatment, while I am relaxed and lucid, the therapist takes my head in her hands and we both meditate for a moment—a tantric moment in which we share a reciprocal healing. Sometimes one or the other of us will "see" or intuit something one of us needs to work on in our spiritual or personal development. Last week, coming out of our brief meditation, I *saw* the thousand-petaled lotus for the first time. Let me explain.

In some Eastern religions, each of us is represented as having a thousand-petaled lotus blossom nestled in our cranium—the crown chakra. It is believed that we come into this life with our lotus closed, the petals acting as veils preventing us from "opening up" too quickly. In essence we are actually the bulb at the center, at once protected and confined by the thousand petals/veils. The purpose of our lives, according to tradition, is to smooth each petal out horizontally, making them into a floating bed, not a prison.

Coming out of meditation last week, I saw the thousand-petaled lotus for the first time; saw that it actually represents the thousand laws governing reality. Each petal represents a single hologram of an entire reality. As we survive our lives, our realities are revealed as illusory, each corresponding hologram collapses, and its petal lies down. Our purpose on this earthly plane at this time is simply to witness the collapse of each hologram, to let go of *all* reality.

Now my reason for including the above incident is because of that word "hologram" that keeps cropping up throughout this writing. My understanding is that the Sirians are the purveyors of the holographic universe—they supply the light forms. But I have to admit, until now I had a sort of Disneyland idea of just what a hologram is. With more and more of the weight of my understanding going to holograms, I became curious. I felt like I needed to know more. The universe/the Brothers/God, recognized my need.

The very next day I was sitting in the dentist's office, waiting to have my mouth rebuilt for reasons I won't bother to explain here. (Let's just say that, about some things, I'm just not smart.) Anyway, I was sitting in the dentist's office, browsing through a random selection of books and magazines, when two books caught my eye: *The Dancing Wu Li Masters* by Gary Zukav, and Michael Talbot's *The Holographic Universe*; unlikely reading matter for a dentist's waiting room. I figured they had to have been put there by God/the Creator. So I spent the next couple of hours scanning both books before going under the knife.

When I came out God told me to steal both books.

I did, and subsequently returned them.

But that night I pored over them until the late hours, fell asleep, woke up just before dawn and put the following together. We have God, Gary Zukav, my dentist, and Michael Talbot to thank.

THE HOLOGRAPHIC UNIVERSE

> If you were to stand behind a master weaver as he works his loom, you would see, not cloth, but a multitude of colored threads from which he picks and chooses with his expert eye, and feeds into the moving shuttle. As you continue to watch, the threads blend one into the other, a fabric appears, and on the fabric, behold! A pattern emerges.
>
> —*The Dancing Wu Li Masters*

No theory created at any level is correct in an absolute sense at all levels. All are only approximations, containing some of the truth but not all of it. The holographic model is simply one more map we chose to chart territory that is both infinite and indivisible. The advantage of the hologram is that it utilizes both hemispheres of the brain at the same time. According to Michael Talbot it works something like this:

A hologram is a three-dimensional image created by light, a *virtual* image that appears to be where it is not, and possessing no more extension in space than does the image you see of yourself in a mirror. Yet you can walk all the way around a hologram and on each side it gives the appearance of having depth. What appears to be a tangible, visible, audible world, is an illusion. It is dynamic and kaleidoscopic, but not really there; that is, *"out there."* Our world and everything in it—from mountain lilacs to the moon—are simply images projected from a level of reality beyond space and time, beyond any so-called laws of physics.

In a holographic universe *all* appearances are illusions, images; not just images created from nothing, but images constructed by the intersection of consciousness with *something*—call it God, call it waves of energy, patterns of motion, intent—*some thing* that is there but beyond human comprehension.

The picture of reality you carry around in your brain is not a true picture at all, but a reflected image. Objective reality does not exist, at least not in the way you believe it exists (you cannot eliminate yourself from the picture). What is out there is really a vast resonating symphony of wave patterns, waves of frequency that transform into the world as you know it only after they enter your senses; after they have been altered and molded by your own *conscious intent*.

The mind is mathematical; the brain is a reduction lens, focusing reality into mathematical strategies, constructing "hard" reality by making *objects out of frequencies*. These mathematical constructs make blurred potential into sound and color and taste and smell. If the brain did not function as a lens, the world of reality would be organized by frequency—no space, no time, just events. The universe is a giant, *living* hologram, fundamentally indivisible. You and I are holographic in nature; your awareness, your feelings, your consciousness, and all your emotions are holographic.

The brain itself is a hologram, interpreting a holographic universe. Individual brains are elements of the greater hologram. Any attempt to separate the universe into parts and particles by naming them is just a convenience, a concession to the brain's three-dimensional function. Cats, dogs, trains, trees, flowers, stars, electrons, quarks, and quanta are just names given to certain aspects of the living universe—as if naming the ears, tail, and paws of a dog somehow separates them from the dog. They may not be the whole dog but they are certainly part of it. And from any one of its parts, the whole dog is implied. Likewise, if you were to break a holographic film into pieces, each portion of it would contain a complete blueprint of the entire film. No matter how broken into fragments a hologram may seem to be, each piece can be used to reconstruct the entire image. As Talbot says, the whole is in every part.

Your mental processes are, in effect, made of the same stuff as the organizing principle of the universe/the Creator. The world of matter, as you think of it, is simply a hologram created by the interaction of consciousness and intent. When the wave form of this flowing hologram, the universe, is observed by conscious intent, a picture is taken of that moment, causing everything in that moment to coalesce into a single, fixed reality; a hologram with past, present, and future fixed around your intent and governing that moment forever. But only that moment.

The laws of one moment do not necessarily apply to the next. Likewise, a picture of that same moment taken by two different observers with different intent, will generate a different hologram, fixed with different realities, drawing different conclusions. Any dimensional shift occurring within a hologram is simply the vibrational variance of your own conscious intent when observing the hologram. You see what you want to see. The universe is what you think it is. And every time you change, the universe changes.

So, what does that say about the *fixed laws* of anything?

There aren't any.

The laws of physics, so called, aren't fixed at all. They aren't even laws. They are simply habits of thought, the single pattern of a hologram done again and again until it becomes a habit, belief in a certain way of thinking held for so long it appears to be immutable. The laws of physics are just one program in the cosmic computer, but a program repeated so often it has become one of *nature's habits*.

The human condition/species is another one of nature's habits. The individual human being is a holographic universe in miniature: unique, self-contained, self-generating, and self-knowledgeable. The tangible reality of your everyday lives is like a holographic image. Underlying it is a level of reality that gives birth to all the objects and appearances of your physical world, the way a single cell of a hologram gives rise to the whole thing. Your thoughts can cause shadowy holographic images to form in your energy fields, and, if repeated often enough and with enough intensity, they can alter the subtle energetic fields of reality itself. Emotionally charged thoughts, such as those accompanying moments of crisis and transformation, are potent enough to manifest miraculous "coincidences" in physical reality—healings, premonitions, prophetic insights, and so on.

In a holographic universe, says Karl Pribam, writing in *Psychology Today*, time is an illusion and reality is a mind-created image. It isn't that the world of images and appearances is wrong; it isn't that there are not objects out there, at one level of reality. It's just that if you look deep enough to penetrate the appearances, you arrive at a different reality, a number of different realities, each one as real as any other. The holographic universe is created by the imagination, but is as ontologically real as is physical reality. Likewise, the future is not set, but is plastic and subject to change.

According to Michael Talbot, reality is a giant hologram, and in it, the past, present, and future appear to be fixed, at least to a point. But that is not the only hologram. There are many such realities floating around out there, timeless, spaceless, each of them fixed in their own past, present, and future—*parallel* universes, jostling and swimming around like so many amoebas.

The future of any given hologram *is* predetermined; when a person has a precognitive glimpse of the future, they are simply tuning into the future of that hologram. Occasionally these jostlings actually jolt you into premonitions. And when you act upon a premonition and appear to alter the future, what you are really doing is leaping from one hologram to another. There are many separate holographic futures, and you choose which events are going to manifest and which are not by leaping from one hologram to another. It is your capacity to *leap* that makes you free, free will creators of your own destiny. Despite appearances, we are beings without boundaries.

—from the Journal, August, 1996

Spirit and Matter

This next was prompted by a conversation with a friend of mine. My friend was struggling through the loss of a relationship; struggling with anxiety and fear, the sense of abandonment that goes with giving up a "personal" love/goal for something deeper and more profound that had not yet made itself known. The conversation started out being very desperate and needy, and ended up with a kind of sweetly laughable "heartsurround" that surprised both of us. I thank my friend for the insights we stumbled upon that night and for the words that found us both, wherever they come from. (The Brothers at work again?) In retrospect, the words sound a lot like what I remember of Thadeus Golas. About twenty years ago I read his book, *The Lazy Man's Guide to Enlightenment*. Thank you, Thadeus, for your part in whatever this is.

The universe is huge and scary and complex on the one hand, but it is also benevolent and so simple in design that there's no reason for anyone to be confused or unhappy.

Understand, the universe is made entirely of one kind of whatever-it-is, which cannot be defined. Don't even try. It's not necessary. All you need to know is that spirit and matter are opposite expressions of that same whatever-it-is, spirit being fully expanded, matter being fully contracted.

And the essential difference between any two beings in the universe, indeed, the difference between dimensions or levels of awareness, is their ratio of expansion and contraction. Expanded beings are permeative; contracted beings are dense. There is no hard wall separating one dimension or level of awareness from another. Each of you alone or in combination, may appear as space, energy, or mass, depending on the degree of expansion or contraction you choose to express.

And each being controls his own.

(There are no victims here. Nothing can be done to you without your cooperation.)

A completely expanded being is space, a level that anyone can reach, but one that is difficult to talk about on this contracted plane. Expansion is experienced as awareness, understanding, enlightenment, love, bliss. At the level of full expansion we are all in the Pool, One Mind together.

Contraction, on the other hand, is felt as fear, pain, anger, hatred—all that. A contracted being feels separate and alone, a victim, unable to choose even the content of his own consciousness. You can go from being a contracted being to an expanded being by letting go of all resistance to what you think, see, or feel; stop judging whatever it is. If you do not like where you are in the universe, just know that you got here by your own decision to expand your heart or withdraw it.

In facing any problem the only question you need ever ask is, should I *expand* to meet this situation, or should I *contract*? Embrace or repel? Open my heart or cross my legs? Am I best served by expanding into love or withdrawing into fear and anger? It's that simple: expand or contract.

Of course if you prefer an image to reality, and by that I mean, if you ask the universe to show you the *who, what,* and *why* of your predicament, the universe will oblige by presenting you with an endlessly detailed horror movie of who, what, and why; image after image, forever, without resolve.

You will, no doubt, manage to convince yourself that you are only suffering through your karma. Maybe so, maybe not.

Karma and Reincarnation

Karma and reincarnation are both mental constructs, not intended to punish but to educate and bring us into balance. They are created at the fourth dimension and played out on the third.

Everything a person experiences is determined by his or her soul, which reincarnates from one body to the next, generating not only the behavior but a holographic template that guides the form and structure of the body itself, the physical attributes necessary for that soul's development. The human body is just an image, another construct, created by thought, created by you to meet your soul's needs. Personal responsibility, not chance, determines your fate.

In order to become whole, the soul must balance its energy. It must experience the effects it has caused. The energy imbalances in the soul are the incomplete parts of the soul that form the personality.

Between incarnations you go to a light-filled place to rest, regroup, and sketch out the important events and circumstances you will encounter in the future. This is done by reviewing all of your actions as seen through *their* eyes, the person on the other end of your actions. You already know how *you* felt, thinking, saying, and doing what you did. Now experience what the other person felt in each of those moments. It is by this measure that you decide what you'll do in the next life, choosing to be reborn with people you have wronged in some previous life in order to make amends. You also plan encounters with individuals with whom you have built loving and beneficial relationships over many lifetimes. You program "accidental" events to fulfill still other lessons and purposes. There are no coincidences, no mistakes, and no victims. The life situation of every human being is appropriate and by design. And all of it is determined by you of your own free will.

There is always free will. The future is only roughly outlined and subject to change; at a very deep and subconscious level, you constantly create circumstances and draw people into your lives that you need to learn from, creating your own reality as you go.

Your deep Self is that portion of you that can see the parts of the future that are predetermined. It is the part responsible for creating your destiny. But it is not alone in this process. Your hopes, fears, dreams, and imaginings do not vanish after leaving your mind, but are turned into thought forms, and become the stuff from which the deep Self weaves your future.

Some of you, most in fact, actually program tragedies or life-threatening illnesses into your pattern in order to force you to wake up, to change the complexion of your soul and thus break through to deeper and more positive meanings. You may also program miraculous healings into your pattern. Your own deep self knows precisely what you need, not to keep you happy, but to evolve your inner Self.

People in grosser states of consciousness do not always feel the repercussions of karmic law as quickly as those on the spiritual path. Those who know bear a greater responsibility because they have a greater awareness of what is right and wrong action, and the slightest deviation from the way sets the law in operation.

But there is no karmic retribution. You are not cosmically punished for your sins, so called. In fact, there is no cosmic judgment nor any divine system of punishment and reward. The "law," if you want to call it that, is inside of you. The only judgment that ever takes place is *self*-judgment. Judgment is a function of the personality, and, whether you judge a thing good or bad, right or wrong, it always returns to you as karma. That doesn't mean that you should not act appropriately given the circumstances in which you find yourself. It simply means that you should respond to them with compassion, but without judgment—you never know what healing might be attached, and for whom. From the viewpoint of the soul, no judgment is ever appropriate.

Karma is simply the law of cause and effect, the necessary structure of any creative act. There can be no one-sided reality; when you create something, anything, you also create its opposite. In order to experience your own creation fully, you must experience all sides of it.

However, as soon as you realize that there is neither good nor evil in any person, thing, or condition, in that moment, the *surrendering* begins;

and that leads to the setting aside of karmic law, replacing it with a life lived by grace. (*Grace*, a common expression of the higher dimensions, visited occasionally and seemingly by miracle on the fourth and third.)

But, in order to set aside karmic law, you must first recognize that it does exist at some level, that the evil you think or do reacts upon you. This realization prevents you from blaming somebody or some circumstance for any predicament in which you find yourself. You begin to see that you, alone, are responsible.

That said, keep in mind that karma is created by the god-realm of the fourth dimension and played out on the third dimension, but has *no relevance at the fifth*. The fifth is a service dimension, the dimension of light/Christ-consciousness. From the fifth dimension on, karma is meaningless and inoperative. To be "karma-free," is to have your consciousness *centered* in the fifth dimension, or above, no matter what level—third or fourth—you happen to be operating on. Most of you are here to assist planet Earth in her ascension from the third to the fourth. But you are actually *of* the fifth.

If you are still holding to a paradigm of linear evolution, a system of conflict and impact, of cause leading to effect; if you think evolution favors the strongest, the fittest, the most intimidating, *get over it*. That's a dying paradigm. The current and ongoing increase in violence and domination is simply the death throes of that paradigm, movement of the human species through its own negative thought-forms collected in the fourth dimension. But reality itself is changing. Your vibrating consciousness is causing it to change. *Resonant causation* is replacing mechanical causation. The entire planet, and with it the human species, is preparing for an evolutionary leap of quantum proportions.

Quantum. Beyond space and/or time. If you are just getting familiar with the concepts of "karma" and "reincarnation," don't get too comfortable. Your comfort zone is about to be challenged again. We are coming to the end of the karmic day, and everything is about to change.

Reincarnation is another aspect of the soul's development. Its primary function is to allow you to experience all sides of all situations, every role, every mother's son and daughter; this, in order to learn compassion. Compassion: the allowing of thought, feeling, and action in another that you would not allow in yourself, and to do so without judgment. Compassion is not an emotion; it is a way of being. But the path to compassion is through your heart, and only an awareness of your feelings can open your heart. Reincarnation makes that awareness possible by allowing you to live through every experience of the human condition. Having compassion in your heart of hearts, you are able to rise above the illusion of separation and duality.

Reincarnation itself is simply a linear-time based interpretation of *spirit* taking up residence in physical bodies. Ego is the overseer of spirit-in-body, and views these "residences" as occurring in a progressive manner. Understanding the concept of multiple realities occurring in simultaneous time allows you to perceive incarnational lifetimes as not just linear, but also parallel. Your spirit has the potential to fragment into bodies and lifetimes that are not just past, present, and future, but parallel and simultaneous. You can literally have an incarnational aspect of yourself that is a simultaneous self from a concurrent other-world reality, or a future self projecting into a simultaneous position in order to make contact with you—a message from the future. That's where the Brothers come in. And angels. They are really aspects of your future, sent here by you, to remind you of all this.

Of course angels, the Brothers, karma, quantum, holograms, self creating self, these are all difficult concepts to accommodate when you are working through a dense three-dimensional body with a brain designed to filter reality into linear segments. If, in fact, your sense of time is linear, with linear processing, then it could take *forever* to transform your cellular structure, and thereby "create your own destiny." On the other hand, in a multidimensional universe, all reality is simultaneous, and all time is now.

ANGELS

Speaking of angels, I was told that we created them. Indeed, they are us, we are them. Anybody who has spirit is an angel. It's just a matter of which side you choose to walk on. (Unless you choose to walk a double path.) You already have knowledge of eleven densities; the angel realm is just one. You only need to wake up and remember them.

Before the inception of this human project, we created a race of angelic messengers to awaken us when the time was right. Created by our own intent, they represent our original state of unified awareness before we entered matter and became a part of this ongoing experiment. Their value, as well as their limitation, lies in the fact that they have no comprehension of the *process* of our undertaking. They know *what* we are doing, but not *how*, and probably not *why*. In that way, they are able to serve without judgment. As an aspect of our divine nature, they are not above or beyond us on some hierarchical scale of evolution. Indeed, they actually envy us the full range of our experiences on this material plane. For that reason alone, they are eager to come here and serve in whatever capacity. Their job is simply to observe the goings on, and occasionally remind us of who we really are. Sometimes they do this from the outside; sometimes they awaken us from within, but always at our darkest and densest hour, when we need most to be reminded that we are not alone or separate.

THE SURRENDERING

The ego regards any change as threatening, whether that change be in the personal self or the world you have created around you. Faced with change, the ego solicits help from the intellect, and together they drag your mind up and down countless avenues of thought and thinking, distractions designed to put the ego back in control. The heart, listening to the mind and finding no answers, no safe haven, becomes fearful and eventually closes.

Personal transformation requires that your heart be kept open and your mind still. Most of you are in the habit of doing just the opposite. Your sense of separation, anger, and fear comes from the mind's incessant chatter, depending on the ego/intellect to rationalize, read, or otherwise think your way through a problem. When this fails, the heart shrinks back in fear. It is your own mind that causes your heart to close. And when the heart is closed, the universe can nourish neither it nor you.

It would seem that the key to expanded awareness is *surrender*.

Most of you think that it is by your own personal efforts and motivation that you have come so far, and by those same efforts you will, "by God," go further. Nonsense, I am told. Effort interferes with the process of awakening. There is only one thing that you need do that you are not already doing, and that is to surrender and accept. Stop trying to manipulate your circumstance. Stop trying to win. There is everything to gain but nothing to win. Give up your attachment to cause and effect, pain and pleasure, one dimension over another, any self-promoting or self-defeating hierarchy of consciousness. Give it up. Stop thinking that you need to be somewhere else doing something else. Accept that wherever you are in this moment is exactly where you are supposed to be.

You do have free will, but the ultimate act of that free will is to surrender your *personal* will to *divine* will; all you are really giving up is the *illusion* of being in control. You've *never* been in control, not in any "personal" sense, at least.

And don't make the mistake of thinking that an act of surrender is something you do once and it's done. Surrender is ongoing. You must surrender your personal will again and again in increasingly subtle ways. You may have to go through being broken in two. You will certainly go through every thought and every fear that has authority over you: your fear of betrayal, fear of abandonment, fear that if you do give up your will to God/ the Creator you will suffer terribly, you will be alone and broke, your sex life will go out the window, your life will be horrible, and so on. Until, finally, exhausted and burnt out from working within the realm of personal will and human limitations, you give up, saying, all right, you win, I'll do it your way; at least with the divine there are no limitations.

At the point where you have surrendered all your fears and all your resistance, and can honestly say that it is more trouble to hold on to the external world than to let go, when you are willing to relinquish faith in anything and everything less than God, even to the point of giving up faith in the God the world thinks it knows, at that point you shift easily and suddenly into a dimension of grace, a dimension that appears to be physical but with less density and more light. You, yourself, become more energy than matter. The rules at this point are to play honestly, play with integrity, abandon hope, and live trusting the time and manner in which your life unfolds.

At this level of surrender you may become an instrument for the universe, serving when, where, and in whatever capacity the Creator sees fit; you surrender your energy, your entire circuitry to *unconditional service.* You may even become a channel for processing negativity that other people can't handle, processing for the collective populace. In which case, you may suffer bouts of ill health and fatigue that are not yours at all—an act of free will, but from the highest level of service and surrender.

And if you think "service" has anything to do with where you are employed or how you make your living, think again. At this level, it is possible for you to serve from the spirit without having to show up in the physical body to help the object or event of service. From the privacy of your own life, your own room, you can send your energy and *know* that it has 100 times more influence than sending your body; you begin to operate at the level of spirit, surrendering your will to divine use, for the good of all—unconditional service, done impersonally and without regard for or expectation of its outcome, serving the moment that is put before you, whatever that moment contains.

Of course, I wanted to know what is meant by "abandon hope." That seems contradictory to living a life in pursuit of the God within, or any god for that matter. What else can we hold on to while we search for that illusive god, if not hope?

First of all, I was told that hope takes you out of the moment; you *hope* things will be better tomorrow; you *hope* your life will be different; you hope your wife will be smarter, your husband more sensitive; you hope, at some time in the future, your neighborhood, your town, and the world in general will be as safe as they were yesterday, years ago. All of these little "hopes" do two things: they assume a negative, and they take you out of the moment, which is all that really exists.

Faith, on the other hand, is another matter; faith *knows,* in this moment, that everything is as it should be, and if it needs to change, it will change.

The value of desperation and any real emergency is that it hardens up the muscle of your faith at the same time it allows you to dump nonessentials. And hope is one of the nonessentials that needs dumping. It's like carrying too much fat around the heart. Not faith, mind you. You could all use more faith. But hope has absolutely no value.

Beneath the surface of hope is an underpinning of doubt, a lack of faith, implying that you're not at all sure about the order and system of things in the universe, that maybe God/the Creator has made a mistake, that perhaps you know better what you need than the Creator does. And way in the back of your brain you're not entirely convinced that things will ever get any better. So you *hope* that they do and *doubt* that they will.

The lesson in this is simple but difficult to do: follow your own inner guide from moment to moment. Tomorrow will take care of itself. A life in the past or the future cannot be shared with the present. Each person who gets stuck in time gets stuck alone.

And while you're letting go of unnecessary things, consider this: enlightenment is the final nightmare, the ultimate bondage, thinking you need to *know* more in order to *be* more.

In truth, one more seminar won't do it; one more teacher won't do it; reading one more book, or sitting at the feet of one more master won't change who you are. At some point, you will just run out of gas (or money) and simply have to go inside and surrender.

Pursuit of enlightenment causes the palms to sweat, the heart to skip, the mind to become tentative, unsure of itself; it is just another way for the ego/intellect to control who you think you are. Meanwhile, joy goes out the window, and with it any real sense of liberation.

Let go of who you think you are, any idea of specialness. Being special means being separate; to think that you are not already enlightened reduces the idea of enlightenment to just another fantasy in the mind. It is ego's way of planning and attending its own funeral.

—from the Journal, August/September, 1996

THE PIANO DREAM

The rest of the summer was hot and nasty.
After my initial surge of health and well-being,
some anomalies began to creep in. Each morning I
woke up with a new pain in a different place. And
not just general neuralgia either. My brain ached.
My ears ached. Most of September I had diarrhea.
By October I had such severe gastrointestinal
reflux that the Brothers decided to schedule me for
opening-heart surgery. All of it, the direct result of
a massive downloading of light into my cells, or so
I'm told, inconvenient but not uncommon.

I once had a friend who, while plowing his
back lot, cut through a power line, shooting him
twenty feet into the air, singeing all the hair on his
body, including the hair on his tongue, and knock-
ing him unconscious. After about a minute he
came to, jumped up, jumped back on his tractor
and spent the next eighteen hours doing the work
of six men, and doing it easily. Afterwards, he said
it was the clearest, most lucid day of his life. Of
course he suffered the loss of some brain cells, and
he was so sore the next day he couldn't get out of
bed, but all in all, he was none the worse for it.

That's the way I felt: blessed and cursed in the same instant by the same deed.

And my dream life was amping up as well: more detailed, and absolutely bizarre. I began to revisit and rethink dreams I've had in the past, some of them recurring for years. This next event is one of those.

It actually started several days earlier when an old and useless anger welled up inside of me and I couldn't identify it or determine where, in fact, it was coming from. Angry, bitter, and miserable, I did what anyone else would probably do. I blamed it on my environment: my wife, my family, my friends. I even resurrected an old enemy or two just to have something or someone to hang it on. And when that didn't work, I blamed it on God. God. I seemed to have a worm in my soul, and I didn't know what to do about it.

This was the first day of November, the first freeze, and I left work early, walking into a mix of ice and rain. The ground felt bony and brittle underfoot, and I walked, trying to *think* my way into some sort of solution, or at least a clearer understanding of the problem. At home I stamped and slammed around all evening, talking to myself in such an abusive manner that my dog took it personally. I watched television with the sound off until my wife grew irritated and went to bed. Finally, around midnight, I drank a glass of milk, and went to bed myself.

Restless and fitful, I slept for an hour or two, dreamed at some point that I was playing the piano, and woke up for good at 2:22 A.M. I took my pillow and moved into the living room, tried to meditate, and couldn't. So I read, started this journal entry, then turned the light out, opened the curtains, and lay back on the couch. It had begun to snow. In fact, it had probably been snowing for hours.

So I lay there watching the snow fall past the streetlight on the corner, and thinking about my piano dream. It was not the first time I've had this dream or something like it. With different settings, different circumstances, and different facts, I've been having this same dream for over twenty years. Truth is, I used to daydream about playing in a band, of playing the piano and being popular at parties. In school I was always awkward and alone. Everybody thought I was being aloof. But I wasn't. I'd go to parties and stand in a corner staring straight ahead, pretending to have deep thoughts. It was a con. I would pick out an empty spot in the room and stare myself right into it. I imagined myself to be the piano player in some deep, dark jazz hole, sort of a cross between Franz Liszt and Bill Evans just bursting with genius and passion and . . . what? Cocaine, I guess. I was willing to give up life, love, and my religion for whatever it was I thought they had.

I continued to lie there on the couch, watching it snow, the edges of my thought getting softer and softer, my mind drifting into a calm, meditative silence; passing moments pooled together, relaxing into one; distinctions between inside and outside dissolved.

Gradually I became aware that something in the room had changed. Something was different about the room itself. It took awhile for me to realize that it was the furniture. And the walls. Even the window hangings were different. I seemed to be lying on my couch looking at my same room with different furnishings and different walls. Actually, I was not so much in both rooms at once as I seemed to be lying on the couch looking into both rooms at once. Odd, I thought, interesting; I wonder what it means. And even as I wondered, a third room began to take shape in front of me, the same room with still different furnishings. I seemed to be lying on the couch, looking into the same room furnished three different ways, simultaneously. Three different dimensions, I wondered?

But before I could wonder any further, I got up and went to the piano. It is an old upright grand, a piece of furniture actually, abandoned to my wife by a relative, but never played. I sat down at the piano and made an easy melody. I like it, I thought. I like the way it sounds. More than that, I like the way it *feels*. I began to elaborate on the melody, my fingers running up and down the keys. And as I played I looked out the window to the streetlight below where a young man and woman stood huddled together, their breath visible in the night air. I watched them and I played without thinking. The music was the only movement. It filled the room but went unnoticed by the couple in the street. I played and did not think of my wife sleeping in the room down the hall.

It occurred to me that I do not know how to play the piano; indeed, that I have never before played a piano in my life. I don't know one note from another. In that moment, however, it didn't seem to matter. I seemed to be relying on some hidden memory that grew as I played. At that level, my knowledge was real, the playing was real, the melody strong and pure and full of resonance, and the whole thing driven by *intent*. As long as I kept my fingers moving and didn't stop to think about it, I could play. And I did play. Wonderfully, gloriously, with more and more passion and abandon.

And as I played, someone identical to myself sat down at the piano and began to play. The other someone looked to the street below, noticed the couple huddled together, looked away, and did not think of my wife. He played the same melody on the same piano, but played it slightly better than I did. And as he played, a third identical someone sat down and played the piano. Indeed, there was a fourth and a fifth, like an image caught in facing mirrors there were a countless number of identical selves sitting in their rooms playing pianos, and an infinite number of wives not being thought of at the moment; but there was only one couple, and one melody, played again and again.

We were playing and writing notes down on a blank piece of sheet music at the same time. Fantastic. We were projecting all the tones within the space of one octave and then sketching them together at weird and specific angles. When we finished sketching them together, we had something that resembled the shape of a leaf. We were reading the leaf and playing the piano when my wife came down the hall in her nightgown.

"What's all the racket?" she said. "Turn off the damned radio and come to bed."

"The radio's not on," I said. "You're dreaming again. Go back to sleep."

Suddenly it was morning and the dream was over. Without a moment's hesitation I went straight to the piano and sat down. Now, understand, I still couldn't play the piano. I know nothing about music and even less about leaves. But I did manage to finger and chord my way through the melody I'd been listening to and playing all night long.

Of course that first piano dream was over twenty years ago. At the time, I considered the melody to be no more than an odd sidebar to an enjoyable if very unusual dream. I've had a similar dream perhaps a dozen times since, always accompanied by the same melody. However, this is the first time I've had the dream since my onboard experience a few months ago.

When I got up the next morning it was, literally, a new day. I felt relaxed, refreshed, *innocent of mind*. The anger I'd carried around for days was gone. I had no more idea about its content than I'd ever had, but I felt suddenly relieved of its burden. I went immediately to the piano and sat down. After twenty years, I'm afraid I'm not much better than I was that first time; it still has to do with my being able to surrender to the playing without thinking about it. But—and this is the point, if there is one—something in the playing this time, something in the progression of three or four chords, the *only* three or four chords, triggered a sudden and deep emotional response. More than that, it caused my heart to break open, the *compassionate heart* that lies almost comatose somewhere in the region of my thymus. My heart broke open in this wonderfully painful way, causing me to cry, and seeming to lift me right up and out through the top of my head, experiencing what I can only describe as "grace," an *awful* grace.

The Brothers were everywhere, touching me, holding me, their electrically charged hands thrust deep inside my heart, bony fingers of light performing some sort of surgery, causing me to be open and available in that instant to all things wonderful and all things terrible. I cried. Not a lot, but enough to know that this was only the beginning of something.

It was clear that the gears of heaven were shifting. And I was about to access some deep, previously unsounded aspect of myself/my compassionate heart, opening me up to *what*? One can only guess.

(Of course where God and the Brothers are concerned, it's not necessary to guess. One has only to have patience, and be willing.)

—from the Journal, November 1-4, 1996

Message from the Greys?

Not long after my initial onboard experience, I began to see things differently—more things, new things; both my range and angle of perception changed/seemed to change. It's not that I am suddenly able to *see* in any psychic sense, so much as I seem to *know* things for the first time, new things I hadn't really given much thought to before; a thought-form will come in with a piece of this or a piece of that. Occasionally, an entire paradigm will come in, with its own values, its own boundaries and its own perspective—how accurate or complete it is, I have no way of knowing, but it certainly is detailed. This next event was like that. It was disturbing at first, not so much in what it had to say as in where or *who* the communication seemed to be coming from. And it was almost like taking dictation.

This has to do with an alien civilization, thought to be extraterrestrial, and known as the "greys" (a mis-identification, I would find out later). Before this incident, I had a limited interest in the greys, and no hard information. I knew they were suspected of being responsible for cattle mutilations all over the world, perhaps even the abduction of a number of Earth's citizens. In 1995, pictures showing the autopsy of one of these beings was shown on television around the world. The gray, hairless body with a small head and distended abdomen was claimed to be that of an alien who had crashed to earth in a flying saucer near Roswell, New Mexico, in 1947.

I can't confirm or deny any of that. It's just not the sort of information I am privy to. And that would seem to be an entirely different civilization than the one I was being made to listen to. You be the judge.

After my onboard experience, I immediately wanted to know what the greys had to do with it. Paranoia and local folklore had led me to believe they were probably responsible for most of the abductions taking place.

Nothing, I was told. The greys had nothing to do with your onboard experience. They are watching, they are curious, but they do not have the requisite equipment to interfere. The stargates to higher dimensions were intentionally designed to require emotion in order to pass through them. Intellect can't do it; nothing of the mind alone. That experience requires a momentary *balance* of heart and mind for it to take place. The greys are predominately mind, with no real feeling nature. An intact feeling nature is necessary to make any sort of dimensional shift such as took place when you were called onboard. They would like to understand it. They would like to be a part of it. They view your ability to shift dimensions as your salvation. But they are genetically denied that experience.

I didn't understand what any of that meant, but it was enough for me. I put the greys to rest and didn't give them much thought after that.

Until now, nearly a year later, when they suddenly came flooding back into my consciousness in a way that I could not have anticipated or deny. What follows is part of a transmission that seemed to emanate from some deep, previously unacknowledged part of myself.

First, let me tell you that this episode followed directly on the heels of a dream, another recurring dream that's been with me for as long as I can remember, and I'm not at all sure what it has to do with anything. I put these two episodes together because of their sequence, one seeming to trigger the other. If there is any real connection, I'll let you be the one to make it.

I seemed to be on a battlefield with bodies all around and on top of me. Whoever the enemy was, they were methodically moving across the field, seeing to it that everyone was dead, running bayonets through those who weren't. I was one who wasn't. I had it in my mind that if I kept my eyes closed and held my breath, if I made no utterance and did not move, they would either overlook me or they would pierce me with a bayonet and it would make no difference. I had to go deep inside myself and surrender to whatever happened next. If I lived, okay. If I died, that was okay, too. Everything would be fine if I would just lie still and let the next thing happen. Which I did. Even as they ran the bayonet through me, I fell deeper inside myself; I felt no pain, just a mild swimming sensation, briefly, then I came to with a start, still inside the dream. I seemed to be on an operating table under a bright light, surrounded by who or what I don't know. Then I woke up. Back in my bed, in my primary reality, I woke up.

Now I've had a similar dream a number of times throughout my life, always seeming to come awake in the middle of the dream on an operating table. Then coming awake again. The dream always starts out feeling nightmarish but never seems to end that way. The after-effect is not one of fear but of amazement and relief, as though I've been somewhere meaningful and done something worthwhile; the only discomfort is in not being in control. And I am pleased and relieved when it's over.

Could it be that the dream itself is a sort of mask for some surgical procedure, performed by who knows who, disguised to appear like something my mind could at least compute; indeed, whatever the medium, the message seems clear: be still, don't resist, let the next thing happen, you are not in any ultimate danger—that is, your soul is safe no matter what may become of your body.

The only "normal" waking experience I have to compare it to is one, several years ago, in which I was undergoing minor surgery and was injected with sodium pentathol and told to count backwards from 100. I remember counting to ninety-seven and then swimming down and under and out. I woke up an instant later and two hours had passed. The surgery was done and I didn't remember a bit of it. That's what the end of this dream feels like. I've always dismissed the entire episode as some sort of past-life memory, circa World War II, perhaps. Now I'm not so sure.

This night I could not go back to sleep. I got up, ate, tried to read, tried to meditate; finally I dressed and went for a drive.

There is no logic to what happened next.

For about an hour I had been driving around randomly, and, feeling inexplicably homeless, friendless, and without a god, when suddenly I was stricken with an overwhelming sense of compassion for the greys. The greys. It occurred to me that they are simply a companion civilization in the universe, facing the extinction of their entire race, desperate, and without hope. My heart was open to them, and it was this sense of compassion, I think, that triggered this transmission. At least that's what I was told when I asked my own inner guidance.

I was driving around a lake on the edge of the city when my head began filling up with thought-forms. I pulled onto the dam, stopped beneath a streetlight, and made the following journal entry.

We are your future, they said, a race of humanoids come from several million light years in your future. You are the original creation from which we developed. We are your future should you continue in the direction you are presently going.

At the time of early man on Earth, we carried out genetic experiments to provoke evolutionary leaps. These leaps did not allow for soul-infusion or any real spiritual consciousness. Spiritual consciousness is born of suffering; our purpose in taking the path we did, i.e., technology, genetic engineering, all that, was to avoid pain and discomfort. In order to avoid suffering, we created a reality without suffering; a one-sided reality. Suffering opens the door to grace, without which there can be no real joy. We are not unhappy, but neither are we truly happy. We are highly intelligent but something is missing.

We are not born. Our bodies are not sexually reproduced, but created with thought power through the affinity principal. (It seems that they are created individually and have individual awareness, but have no sense of self-purpose. And because they've lost contact with their source, they must be grown and cultivated, not unlike a plant or vegetable. The human species has hope for ascendancy through its own self mastery, they said. However, they do not share that hope because they have no self to master.)

And when we die, when we realize we are about to die, we simply leave our bodies. It's like leaving a car behind that has been wrecked or will no longer run. And because our new bodies are already cloned and waiting for us, we take on new bodies right away, without losing consciousness in the process. However, because we have a limited feeling nature, we have no joy, no hope, no real expectation for the future. We are simply living out our karmic destiny.

Our downfall was in having intelligence enough to anticipate and avoid problems, and choosing to create a life void of pain and suffering. We deviated from the divine principal necessary to evolve as humans do, they said. We envy you your future species as it is envisioned. Learn from us. Steer away from external technology, that which is engineered outside your own bodies. While medicines and some technology are certainly valid, it is not in your best interest to rely solely on externally engineered solutions. You are divinely made and genetically constructed to *become* the technology, to alter your own vibratory state of being from within, enough to alter the consequences of illness and disease as experienced in the third dimension. External solutions are not permanent because they only deal with the symptoms, not the cause. (How many viruses have we "cured" only to find them reappearing now, thirty years later, as new, mutated, and virulent strains for which we have no medicines?) The cause is within you, they said, as is the cure.

External technology, because it has no link with the heart, no real feeling nature, limits one's ability to move between dimensions. Indeed, it may negate it altogether. That is why we are confined to the third and fourth dimensions. Once a path is chosen it must be seen through to its conclusion. One should be aware ahead of time of the path one is taking. The price one must pay to avoid the pain and difficulties of soul-infusion is very high. We would trade with you if it were possible.

While we are genetically made and genetically controlled, they said, we do not believe in a personal God dependent on genes. However we do honor those beings from deep in the universe who live utterly from their consciousness. Some of you are descended from those beings.

We are here by your invitation, they said (my emphasis). We could not interfere with you otherwise. Some part of you wanted this communication. We are not permitted to violate or intrude upon any of you without your permission, and we conduct no experiments intended to cause pain. Your fear is the cause of your pain. For that reason, we do sometimes shield our presence or mask our operations. (There it is: is that what my battlefield dream is about?) We intend no harm, but because we have no measurable fear or pain of our own, we don't always recognize the limits of yours.

Any abduction or violation of your person is carried out by a race of humanoids from your *past*, they said. You call all of us "greys," but we are not the same. What you call "greys" is in fact a race of humanoids from your own past. There is no need to fear them, however; they are receding further into your past. They cannot go where you are going.

Mankind is not a natural creation, but was specially developed to work for a particular group of star creatures—the same beings from whom you are descended. Human beings were created as slaves to work for the gods. They were genetically made for special purposes. However, because of their courage and determination to break their genetic chains and live their lives in freedom, though born as slaves, they were chosen for the *noble experiment*.

The human race as it now exists is a hybrid species in the middle of its own birthing process. You are not complete. Your ongoing birth and creation process is being monitored by a number of civilizations throughout the universe. We are not the only ones interested in your development. You do have free will, they assured me, and that cannot be violated. However, you volunteered in the beginning of this experiment to allow all of us to monitor your birth and development. You are the living prototype for a future race. Some of you are beginning to wake up to all this. You are beginning to remember; however, your memories are fragmented at this time, causing you to become confused and fearful.

You are now at a time in your history when no secret is safe and when all that is lodged in the unconscious will surface. There is great potential for fear, and the need to make choices. Do not let fear determine your choices. What you choose now will determine your reality for a very long time. Your future holds the possibility of many different realities. The safe way is not necessarily the best way.

Your greatest *internal* danger is fear generated by your own emotions. You are never in danger from outside emotions, only from your own.

Your greatest *external* danger lies in the coming polar shifts brought on by changes in Earth's atmosphere as your system moves into a different energetic space. As a result of this "Earth displacement," the planet will transfer to another space density and an entirely new constellation will be created. Indeed, your entire solar system will move into a different part of space creating completely new conditions of space/time which will, in turn, have their affect on the brain cells of the creatures living here; all of them, yourself included. The displacement process is already going on. You cannot stop it. It is part of your evolutionary path. Those who *know* will be protected. You will be shown.

Your next evolutionary step is *immortality within a physical body* (my emphasis). Some of you are ready. Most are not.

A material body is necessary to life. Without a body there is consciousness but no life. God is All-Consciousness, everywhere. *Life*, on the other hand, is a cooperative, co-creative process; it is the experience of differentiated consciousness—one thing from another. To know life, a body must be infused with consciousness. To bring God to life, consciousness must inhabit a physical body.

Wherever you are on any path is to that end. To reject your life is to deny God the experience of being alive. . . .

Now, I'm going to interrupt right here, partly to skip details I couldn't really follow, much less make sense of, but also to catch my emotional breath, and address some reservations.

I had been writing as fast as I could for two hours without questioning anything that came through. However, at a certain point, an instinctive fear took root inside me together with a kind of rational objection to what I was being told. Like I said, I don't really *see* things in any psychic sense; if anything, my abilities are conceptual, words and descriptions that only take form as I am speaking or writing them down. That's a blessing, I guess; not to have to look at everything that is going on. I have a good friend, George, on the other hand, who does *see*. He is my eyes sometimes when I need to verify what I'm being told. He was my teacher's eyes on occasion. I include this next, because it verifies some of what George had been seeing for months and could not make sense of.

In the beginning, it seems, the so-called grey civilization was not too different from the human species except perhaps in their level of intelligence which led them to resist any real *internal* change; they were "too smart" and "too advanced" to be influenced by Spirit. Every technological move they made was designed to avoid pain to them-selves—growing pains, pain of birth, all that; indeed, their earlier experiments in genetic engi-neering were intended to save women the pain and inconvenience of childbirth. Later, again in order to save themselves the risk of injury, whole armies were cloned, then teams of intergalactic explorers were cloned and sent out, and so on. They chose not to "suffer" through soul-infusion by cloning instead, hoping to leap over that evolutionary step. And that has lead them into an evolutionary dead end.

Of particular concern, at least to George and myself, are the *monitoring devices*, light or resonance-sensitive monitoring devices—implants, in other words. Used for tracking purposes, an implant acts like a beacon to higher dimensional beings; they are drawn to it.

Eons ago, it seems, a large number of the human populace volunteered to help the greys understand soul-infusion by allowing themselves to be monitored, *not* controlled. In so doing, this alien civilization—the ones we call greys—hopes to record biochemical/DNA changes in response to stress, pleasure, all things to do with our "feeling nature," which they don't have. They hope to duplicate the changes that take place during the soul-infusion process. Their intention is not to take over our souls, but to duplicate them. Which, of course, they can't; by divine principle, they can not. *And they know this*. Still, they are destined to hope against hope, and do what they do, until the end of their own karmic day.

The problem: dissolution of these devices is made to coincide with our individual awakening. In other words, as we become more light filled and the rate of our resonating consciousness increases, the devices are designed to come to the surface and dissolve. And all of this is meant to take place in the etheric, with no conscious awareness on our part. However, should we become fearful at any time during the dissolution process, say, the anesthetic wears off and we suddenly come to in the middle of a surgery, our fear then causes the vibrations to slow down, the energy around these devices to become more and more dense, and ultimately be trapped in our density. Moving from the etheric to the physical, they become lodged there. It is our fear that makes them manifest and our fear holds them in place. Let go of your fear, they said, and they will dissolve on their own.

When the transmission was over I felt emptied out and peaceful, but exhilarated, like I could run the seven or eight miles home or lie down anywhere and sleep for days. Rather than feeling invaded or violated, I just felt grateful and amazed to be part of whatever was going on. It was the last hour before daylight, and everything was still. The flat lake looked like a black marble slab. I sat for awhile, watching it do absolutely nothing. Then I drove to the end of the dam, away from the lake, and back into the rest of my life.

THE GREAT SHIFT

During the next several days, I slept in fits and starts, mulling over a number of the particulars intimated by the above transmission. I went "inside" and consulted my own divine guidance. Some of what I got was disturbing, and all of it was confusing—by that I mean, my entire belief system/mechanism felt threatened. Again. New information seemed to be coming from everywhere at once.

Use your own discretion; take what works for you, and put what doesn't on hold.

Not the least of my concerns are the polar shifts. It seems that, coincidental to the Earth's magnetic poles moving to new locations, human consciousness will move into another dimension—the fourth or fifth, in this case, depending on who you are and who you are listening to. All agree that the human consciousness is going somewhere it has not been before. And this event is more synchronistic than causal. By that I mean, the changing of human consciousness is just part of what is going on. Every rock, toad, tree, all of humanity, and every elemental thing on Earth is being fitted for a higher light, a renewed program of *return to Source*. All sentient beings will receive this program within their biological family as a whole, when and to whatever degree their individual consciousness is prepared to accept it.

Of course, some of this is already going on; has, in fact, been going on for years.

However, prior to the shift, all hell could break loose—a period of world chaos in which social systems could fail, political systems collapse, financial systems break down, weather will become volatile and stormy, people may go insane. ("Normal" people are especially at risk. If you are one of "us," and you know something absolutely out of the ordinary is going on, then you'll probably be all right—you may be called on to help process for the masses, but you will be all right. Normal people tend to take their lives too personally.)

It is a well-intentioned hell, causing you to drop old habits, old patterns, old relationships of every persuasion that no longer serve your higher purpose. They're going to be torn right out of your hands. And good riddance. Your choice in all this is not one of "whether or not," but "how" you accept this new paradigm. Once done, you will be cleaner and clearer than you have been in any recent incarnation. Some of you may resent this clarity because you will also be transparent. No secret, no lie, no subterfuge will go unnoticed. Naked to the bone and visible. You will live in integrity or you will be humbled.

But don't take it personally. It's not just you it's happening to. This is a global awakening, a direct line home; under the din of noise and activity, the entire planet is hushed and listening.

While this program for return may not insure our ascension, it will certainly give us a window into that event which we did not have before. And it is currently being imprinted into the crystalline structure of our DNA, to be released as a living hologram at the appropriate phases within the worldwide scheme of things, the ascension schematic. This, in order to leave this realm and enter the New Day; Earth, after the shift.

In the meantime, how does one go about preparing for such a calamitous occasion? Well, you could do nothing and let the God Within guide the way. Or, you could prepare yourself mentally and emotionally to accept whatever comes, and let the God Within guide the way. Of course, if you are a survivalist you're going to have to stockpile food and water and toilet paper enough to sustain you for an indefinite period. That's an option, but unrealistic to my thinking. After the transition, everything will be changed. Your consciousness will be changed. The hologram you are living in will have changed, and you will begin to move through the void, the birth of the new consciousness into the fifth dimension, the dimension of Christ-consciousness. From that point on, everything you may have done to physically prepare on Earth will be of no further use to you, not unlike it was when you were born into this current body.

Perhaps the most powerful thing you can do is connect more intimately with the God Within through prayer and meditation. Do not be afraid; remember that you are holy, whole, complete, and perfect in this moment, and whatever you need will be given to you. This is an opportunity, not a burden. Meditate on your lightbody, the energy field of the human being—an energy field created by all living things, the lightbody surrounds us, permeates us, and binds the galaxy together.

The shift itself is organic and will pass without comment and with little or no awareness by most people. As if my existing belief system wasn't already strained, I was told this: In the actual *moment* of the shift, Earth's magnetic field will drop to zero, and the higher light will become so strong and compacted that it will block out the Sun's light. Earth's biosphere will become so compressed that it will get dark and stay dark, pitch black, for as much as three days, during which time everyone everywhere will go into a sort of hibernation. Those of you whose job it is to hold memory, will enter into a theta state and create a magnetic force field, making it possible to record and retain memory for the entire species; this, while the rest of the planet is sleeping through the correction phase of the polar shift. At the end of that time, most everyone will wake up in a new hologram, one with a different memory bank and new ways of being in the world. Most of you will not remember or record a single thing out of the ordinary.

No stress. No trauma. You will simply wake up from what feels like a busy and dream-filled night, and go on about your business. But your "business" will have changed.

What all that means exactly, I haven't a clue. I'm simply telling you what I was told. Take it with a grain of something.

And just when is all this supposed to take place?

I don't know that either. How could I? How could anyone? I don't *want* to know. Too much time spent worrying about the future hinders your spiritual growth. That sort of knowledge, like knowing the precise moment of your death, interferes with your intended purpose on Earth. Stay in the moment; only in the *now* can we make meaningful changes. There is evidence that the polar shift is upon us, could in fact, already be taking place. (Or has it *already* taken place, and we're just beginning to remember it?) Prepare yourself internally now.

If you think the worst thing that can happen is that you or a loved one will be killed, get over it. Realize that this is your reason for being here. The purpose of life at this stage of growth is to move consciously into the next world, the fifth dimension, the dimension of Christ-consciousness. Of course, there are a number of ways to do that. You could die. Death. That's very traditional but it still works. The only difference is, in the past when you died, you stayed dead for awhile, then you came back to complete your purpose on Earth. Here, at the end of the karmic day however, the dynamics are changing. You would probably die, then be reprogrammed and recalibrated, and sent back pretty much where you left off, but move rapidly up in consciousness to be in harmony with the rest of Earth consciousness.

Or you could chose to resurrect. *Resurrection.* In this case, you still die, but you consciously reconstruct your body after death, calibrating it to be in harmony with your reentry. The optimum words here are: "*consciously* reconstruct." But the results are the same.

Of course, you could choose *ascension*, in which case, you do not die, but rather you consciously move into the next dimension and take your body with you. You and your body simply disappear out of this world, pass through the void, and reappear in the next. Practically no one will notice.

The primary difference in any of these is the level of consciousness you take with you. But we all end up in the same place as the same one thing. It's all the same spirit/Spirit.

So why do it one way as opposed to another?

Because we can. Because we have free will, and our purpose is to live *all* of life's possibilities.

THE ASCENSION

Having said all that, having written myself out on the matter, I went to bed not thinking about much of anything, and fell into a deep and peaceful sleep that lasted for several minutes. Until the word "ascension" popped up like a cartoon balloon. *Ascension*. I keep hearing it mentioned. I keep using it myself, but what exactly does it mean? What is involved? Who is eligible for ascension; when do we start, and how long does it take? My mind was suddenly filled with things related and unrelated, and the rest of the night was busy with overlapping dreams that seemed to carry no clear-cut message, nothing I could embrace and say, Aha!

And the Brothers were there, everywhere. I could feel them moving around the edges of my dreams all night long, all of them seeming to talk at once. It just sounded like so much static. Energetically, it felt wonderful, sort of like a party was going on. I enjoyed the company and didn't worry too much about what I might be missing.

In the morning I woke up filled with a strange energy. Wide awake, alert, almost anxious, I got up and went to my couch and lay down.

Suddenly, and without ceremony, I seemed to be back "on board."

All the Brothers from the night before were there, but had settled on a single spokesperson, a voice that sounded suspiciously like that of my former teacher. I won't try to describe it to you for fear of prejudicing the words. Let's just say that his was a voice I had to "get over" when I first met him. In this context however, it was familiar, and I was pleased and comforted to hear it.

You have to understand that my teacher was an entire lightship himself, full of lights and wheels and miracles. However, my own relationship with him was not without difficulties. I was caustic and argumentative in those days, full of fears and anger. It was his job to suck all that wormy anger stuff out of me. And that he did, with kindness, with compassion, in ways that were elevating and humbling in the same instant. He understood about me long before I understood about myself. I once asked him what he thought my job was on the path, and he told me that I should first learn to clean up my own cage. Part of my job, he said, was to accelerate the evolution of consciousness in people. Then he laughed and said, "but don't expect anyone to thank you for it." (My wife took that to mean that my job was simply to move about the planet and irritate people.) He used to cite me as an example to others, saying, "If Bill can do it, by God, you can do it too."

He saved my life. He took me into his heart, and held me closer to the heart of Christ than I had ever imagined possible. In one awe-filled moment he caused me to understand that the living Christ is not a person or a god but an event latent in all of us. He took me into the very heart of that event and set me free. He gave me back to myself by introducing me to his "Boss." The Big Guy. God. For that I am eternally grateful. Even now, I can't talk about my teacher without something in my heart welling up into tears.

This is the ascension, he said. This planet and all species of life on it are being prepared to "move up" a dimension. First and second dimensional life-forms will become third dimensional life-forms. Humans will graduate to fourth dimensional worlds or fifth dimensional oneness, depending on their level of evolution and their intent. Some may move further than that, and some are already working from levels beyond your wildest imaginings. The ascension is already going on, he said. It's been going on for quite some time, and will continue for as long as it takes. As an event, this was planned eons ago according to some vast cosmic timetable and has nothing to do with any local calendar. Earth is currently blessed by the presence of the largest gathering ever of ascended masters, angels, archangels, and extraterrestrials from every corner of the galaxy. They are here to observe, help, guide, do whatever they can as unobtrusively as they can.

I interrupted him right there. I had my own agenda. I wanted to know how karma fit into all this, and reincarnation.

It doesn't fit in at all, he said. The ascension process lies outside the circle of reincarnation. Before ascension can become a probability, all karma must be cleared. You've been working through karma for too long already, many life-times. However, you are coming to the end of the karmic day. If there is anything you've put off, it will have to be dealt with now. That could make this lifetime very intense and unpredictable. For that same reason your collective social structures may become erratic: governments may collapse, banks fail, there may be widespread violence as people clean up the last remnants of their karma. All of this in preparation for the ascension, where all life begins anew, at a new level of consciousness in a higher octave of existence.

I wanted to know what I could do to help myself and others through this process.

More than anything, be kind to yourself, he said, and be honest. No one is ever as good or as bad as they think they are. As forerunners to a divinely human species it is your job to heal the wounds of separation and bring spirit and matter into reconciliation. Start by removing yourselves from your own crosses. Pass no judgments on yourself or anyone else; do not let your ego/intellect put a value on your thoughts, good or bad. And don't be afraid. Fear is the only thing that can hold you back or slow the process down. Fear exists only when you have embraced an illusion of some sort.

He went on to tell me that the planetary ascension will evolve through a series of steps, changing the physical body while merging the body and the spirit into one being, a perfected being of light in a physical body of light—the emergence of the lightbody. As each step is completed, changes that have occurred must be integrated into all areas of the life and the spirit. This process is designed to bring up all your human issues as you progress, each higher level bringing up a deeper layer than the one before it. As each issue emerges, you have the choice to allow the Christ Light to transmute it, or to clear it by using the light technologies that have become available in recent years. Your choice.

But don't take it personally, he said, obviously reading my mind. This is not a personal process, though it may seem like it, affecting you mentally, emotionally, and physically.

"Could you be more specific?" I said, with a growing angst I'm sure he recognized but chose to ignore.

The first several steps are structured for gradual change at all levels, he told me, with regular spiritual awakenings interspersed with physical, mental and emotional changes. After that, you may experience your first descensions of spirit—spirit descending into the body, accompanied by a noticeable spiritual awakening. You may begin to manifest clairvoyance, clairaudience, or a kinesthetic awareness of the energy. Next you may begin to notice body changes in some extreme ways. Aches and pains may occur, even viral syndromes. You may catch a cold every month or so. You will experience headaches as the optic nerve pathways are turned on and the pineal gland becomes activated; or earaches as your transmitters are rewired. For certain you will experience excessive perspiration and diarrhea as you drop density from the cells of your body. Coincidental to all this, you are adding a third strand to your DNA, reconnecting your spiritual selves to your material selves, and causing you to feel somewhat dislocated from time to time. These changes may take two or three years for the human species to work through, more for the planet. Am I being specific enough? he asked, and didn't wait for me to answer.

There is a void space at the end of each level called ego death. It may manifest as depression or a sense of nothingness. Knowing you (meaning me), you'll probably think you've contracted a full blown case of terminal something. This void is to be used as a rest stop before you continue on. It is an integration chamber, an energetic place where nothing exists, and you are able to build a new picture of yourself and your life before you move to the next step.

The next level is about integrating the spiritual changes and the physical changes into your daily life. Relationships are a focus.

It is through relationships that you test yourself and the changes that have been made. You may find that any relationship based on control, manipulation, or fear will become intolerable; many relationships end during this phase. (Note that lifelong marriages are becoming increasingly rare in this present age; we come together for spiritual purposes that may last a few weeks or months or years. When that purpose is served, the union will most likely be altered or severed entirely.) The void that attends this level can be extremely painful. After so much focus on relationships, this void requires you to ultimately be alone with yourself. Indeed, the relationship you have with yourself is the most important relationship you will ever have.

At the beginning of the next level, life feels new; you may feel newly born and tender. This is the beginning of the spiritual awakening in which your abilities, your gifts of the spirit, will become stronger as you become energetically clearer. The focus will be on manifesting these gifts, and then integrating them fully so that they are usable in your everyday life. You will be required to live by your spiritual gifts.

Transition into the next level is so easy that the shift can sometimes go unnoticed. Your spiritual gifts continue to grow, and your physical body begins to change in appearance. Friends may remark that you look younger, or changed in some indefinable way. But this level also brings deeper processing of emotional issues. You'll have to deal with all your beliefs and thought forms around death and loss. You might create disillusionment, or find that you are creating your deepest fears so you can clear them completely by experiencing them. Those same human issues that you thought you'd dealt with earlier will probably come up again, with greater intensity.

Those of you on the front edge of the ascension will realize that you are playing without a safety net—no insurance perhaps, no family support should you become diseased or disabled in some debilitating way. You are on your own. There will be days in which you feel abandoned by God and the very choices that have brought you this far. This is a challenge to go deeper into the Spirit. Stop trying to figure out how you got here, or where it is you're going. Stop trying to *think* your way to the next level. God speaks to the soul in ways that are felt by the heart; the mind is always the last to know. God and your divine self didn't bring you this far just to watch you drown. Trust the miracle that has become your life.

At this level, any energy stored in the emotional or mental body must be released to the spiritual body. If you don't deal with those issues now, at the next level you'll begin to manifest them into your daily existence. Not a fun thing to do, he assured me.

The process of becoming clear is one of releasing energy stored in the emotional and mental bodies, and relocating that energy to the spiritual body where it becomes usable. This is done by first suspending all judgment having to do with your thoughts and emotions; stop thinking of them as good or bad, right or wrong; forget the circumstances surrounding the thought or emotion; let go of the details. Observe them without interacting. Be mindful of each moment, but don't let your intellect assign values.

No judgments. No finding fault or pleasure. Just observe and record. In this way, you not only change the intent of the thought or emotion, you convert the experience of it into raw energy. Then use your mind to move this energy into the heart of compassion to be balanced and purified with light and love. From here you can either store the energy in your spiritual body for use later, or you can let it spill out into your immediate environment as love for all things. It is through this energy that miracles are created.

The only difference between a master and any other man is the location of the energy held within his subtle bodies. An ordinary man has all his energy "locked up," stored in emotions and memories in the emotional body, and in beliefs and thoughts in the mental body. The ordinary man has a flat spiritual body; the demands of thoughts and emotions leave no energy to spare.

All the energy held within a master's subtle bodies is stored in the spiritual body. For a master, the energy associated with emotion flows into the emotional body from the spiritual body *in the moment*, and is released back into the spiritual body once the emotional stimulus has ended. This leaves a master's energy free to use according to his or her will. The spiritual energy is available to a master because it is not consumed by thoughts, beliefs, emotions, and memories. Creation of this undiluted structure in your energy bodies makes it possible to manifest thought into physical reality.

Of course, it's always wise to practice discernment. Everything that you hear; everything you see; everything you touch, taste, and smell; every bit of new information that comes your way; check it against the wisdom of your own intuitive heart.

And be thankful that you have some idea what is going on, and that you've been working to clean and clear your human issues. Imagine what the general public is going through, clueless, anxious, angry, and frustrated, experiencing the same changes as you, but without having first cleared and faced their issues. It all seems so very personal, and hopeless. Some of them will go nuts. Don't go nuts with them. It's important that you realize what is yours and what is not. The universe may ask you to assist others, but rarely will you be required to entirely take on someone else's stuff. Know what is yours, and deal with it. But know what is not yours. Stay centered in your own current. By staying centered *within*, nothing that is not yours has power over you.

Remember, there is a constant flow of divine energy that enters through the top of the head as a thin current of light running through the center of your being, and located in the spine. It is lovingly impersonal as it enters the head; however, it becomes more dense and personal as it sinks deeper into the body. Should life become too dense and too personal, or should the stress of any of your lower chakras become temporarily unmanageable, remember, that same current runs *up* the spine and out through the top of the head, connecting us with the Source. Should you forget your own divine origins, or desire to be free of the turbulence of the third or fourth dimension even while working in them, *stay in the current*, abandon all belief systems, look up, literally through the top of the head, and focus on, and *breathe in*, That/the God within. . . .

By now I was beginning to feel like I'd stolen more chain than I could swim with. Swimming up or swimming down, it didn't matter; I was drowning in information. Overwhelmed.

"So, where is all this going?" I asked. "I mean, is there another way out of here, some way around the above-named shit and glorification? I know you say it's not personal, but there must be something personal to be gained. Why else be doing it? And why me?"

First of all, he said calmly, the ascension has nothing to do with leaving the world, but entering it more completely. It is not a means of escape, but the natural result of surrendering all avenues of escape. Perhaps the most important aspect is the transformation of your physical shell into a vehicle capable of merging completely with your *higher self*, an event timed and triggered by the amount of light you are holding within your cells. I guess that would seem to be personal; the more light you hold in your physical body, the greater the level of spirit you can contain within the body. Toward the end of the lightbody process, just preceding the shift into ascension, you will merge completely with your higher self.

The ascension itself is marked by the movement of the *merkabah* into the heart center of your body. It is your geometric lightbody, most easily identified as a ring or ball of gold light. It is the vehicle of your ascension, and a major initiation— an event that marks the beginning of your personal ascension into a fifth dimensional world of oneness.

Why you? he said. And even as he said the next words something inside me broke apart, some recognition caused me to laugh and cry in the same instant. I mean, here he is ten years later and from the "other side," still reaching out, encouraging me in that inimitable voice, saying, "C'mon Bill, this is the ascension; if you can do it, anybody can."

MERKABAH/LIGHTBODY

Merkabah and lightbody are interchangeable terms, key to the ascension process. Both refer to an energy field that exists around every living thing in the universe. Merkabah simply means *light-spirit-body*; it is the spirit-body surrounded by counter-rotating fields of light, wheels within wheels—Ezekiel's wheels, mentioned in the Bible. It is a vehicle to transport spirit-body from one dimension into another. The vehicle of all vehicles. The Big Bus.

Except that it is not a bus, nor anything so benign. It is the universal pattern of creation; a total paradigm. It can take any form, any color. We each have a lightbody field around us. Once activated, it begins to clear and balance our chakras, leading to whole-brain synchronization. Made from the very fabric of consciousness itself, it is alive and conscious of everything everywhere in the universe, including other dimensions.

But it is relatively dormant until you activate it with your *attention* and your *intent*. Your lightbody will simply exist around your body if your consciousness does not give it instructions: where to go, what to do, i.e., what is it you're working on.

By activating your personal lightbody, you align your own energy fields with those subtle energies of your higher self, making service, health, and spiritual transformation priorities in your life. Creating a magnetic force field around you, your lightbody provides personal protection as the Earth goes through its changes. Indeed, it may be the only means for staying in body and in consciousness during Earth's more apocalyptic changes.

The personal lightbody itself consists of two forcefields, interlocked and counter-rotating in a single space and at such speed that they may appear as a sphere of light. You may experience it as a geometric construct of light, a diamond/crystal, with yourself in the middle (accurate but not exactly true).

My own lightbody experience came when I woke up one night with what felt like severe acid-reflux. This went on for over an hour and eventually evolved into high chest pains. By then I was having trouble breathing and couldn't swallow. I was convinced I was having a heart attack as this continued for another two hours then eased off, and eventually left me feeling exhausted and relieved. I slept. Deep and dreamless.

When I woke up I called my doctor and explained to him what had happened. He asked me to come in for tests that afternoon. I did, and we found nothing. My heart was healthy. Other than my blood pressure being high and erratic, I was fine. We decided it must have been some sort of allergic reaction. I couldn't imagine to what or to whom, but that explanation satisfied me. I went home and didn't think any more about it.

Three days later it happened again. Then again a week later, each time followed by a trip to the doctor resulting in the same diagnosis. Eventually I gave up on the doctor. My blood pressure finally settled down, but the condition continued with unnerving regularity for the next four months. What follows made it tolerable.

One night in the middle of an episode, I became aware of a soft gold light spinning around me, around my entire body. Actually, it seemed to emanate from the core of my being out, creating an energy field within and around me that I can only describe as the Christ-self. (I say that now, but at the time I had no name for what was going on.) I felt peaceful, comforted, almost ecstatic. I was still in physical pain, wondering if I might die from it, but it was all right. Everything was all right. I came to understand that an operation was in progress, an excavation of sorts. The bowl of my heart was being hollowed out, being made larger, deeper, enough to hold the compassionate heart. And this body of soft gold light surrounding me had been activated to hold me in body and in consciousness during the operation.

Don't ask me how, or what any of that means. I don't know. What I do know is that sphere of light has not left me since. It is my lightbody, my own living merkabah. And it seems to emanate from the dimension of Christ-consciousness, the fifth dimension as I understand it, the dimension of non-linear manifestation.

Over the next few months, the work on my heart continued, and I began to understand that love is indeed the key to higher consciousness; nothing of the mind, nothing of the intellect. Our lightbody becomes more alive and accessible as our love for life grows. As we let go and forgive; as we begin to love our enemies; as we are able to see the perfection in each moment with every breath, our own living lightbody begins to function on higher and higher levels. Love is the ultimate emotion and unifying force throughout the universe. Activation of the personal lightbody is based on the sacred geometry of love and compassion. Once activated, it amplifies the energies of the heart, making possible our realignment with Source and creating a sacred space of love and joy around us. It literally is the force field of energy that surrounds every living thing, and activates when a person is in a state of *unconditional love/ service.*

Four months into this surgical education everything came to a halt. It stopped as suddenly as it had started. All the symptoms went away. For good. I mean, that was over three years ago and I haven't had a single episode since. During that four months however, I developed a working relationship with my lightbody that continues to this day.

Use of the merkabah activates synchronicity— what you need, the universe will put immediately in your path—and it makes the ascension process possible by disengaging you from the cycle of karma and reincarnation.

Simply put, the lightbody/merkabah is a system for activating increased levels of communication, a living energy transmitter. And we all have one. One just has to activate it to connect into the grid systems of the Earth, the Christ grid, or any number of higher dimensions. Activation of the lightbody helps to integrate all the selves by removing the veils of separation between levels of consciousness and physical reality; i.e., makes possible the integration of all the separate selves into a seamless fabric of consciousness operating on multiple dimensions simultaneously. Of course, as part of the ascension process, it does not resonate with the more dense emotional frequencies: fear, doubt, anger, all that. For that reason, we are at first given only limited access to the lightbody, and then taught to use it in bits and pieces; this, while the complexion of our intent and our integrity are measured. The purpose of all this is to elevate the species, not send it into perdition. *Intent is everything.*

However, it is not necessary to consciously activate your lightbody in order to ascend. It will certainly bring you into a greater awareness of what is going on, and perhaps help you to be a more active participant, co-creator of your own universe. But we are collective in our consciousness, collective in our soul; this is a collective initiation. What one gets we all get. While our level of participation and awareness, even our destinies, may be different, no one will be left behind.

The ascension can occur at an individual level, within a group, or as part of the collective experience. You will ascend when you are ready, whether you do it alone or as a part of the planetary shift. There is no given time frame for the ascension. At an individual level there are ascensions occurring daily. There are many beings who are incarnate because they have volunteered to serve by testing the lightbody experiment, the "noble experiment." They will be the first to be accommodated into a higher dimension of reality, the first wave. Of course, all this is in terms of focus of consciousness and dimensional placement within the grids. They won't beam up or disappear necessarily.

For the rest of us, the lightbody program will continue until we are ready, and then we will shift. Ascension is not difficult or complicated. It is a change that occurs in an instant, but you are still here. The Sun will still shine and the stars will continue to come and go. Your mortgage won't go away. The difference is your ability to live in and feel joy.

Even the word "higher" is misleading because the point of all this is not to go higher or deeper or faster. It's the ego that needs high and low. The goal of your life is freedom and fulfillment. Fulfillment isn't achieved until you know God as completely as God knows Itself.

The easiest way to verify that ascension has happened is to note the quality of joy in a person's life. Defined as *samadhi*, ecstasy, or rapture, joy is a state of oneness with whomever or whatever you think God is. You may experience it as being your center, or being on your center; it is that clear space you sometimes achieve in deep meditation when the energy is flowing unimpeded and you feel no separation, an absolute oneness with all that is. Whatever brings you to that pleasure or feeling of lightness, and whatever you would define as joy, is your pathway to that state. The beginning of the ascension is when a person begins living life by creating their fantasies as their reality, and finds joy in what they have created.

A group working on ascension has a tremendous advantage because fifth dimensional consciousness is a consciousness of "oneness." In other words, the group is one.

As you increase your vibrational level you will be drawn to small groups of like vibration. You will be drawn, not by deeds, but by intent. Small groups will actually be drawn to higher-dimensional zones.

Working with a group gives each member a chance to learn to relate both as individuals, and from oneness within the group. It creates an enormous synergistic energy—each of you is more powerful than you would be if you were alone.

Islands of Light will form around those who remain here to serve and have raised their vibrations very high. They will create vibratory frequency bands that surround their group, their homes, their vehicles, and places of work. They will be led to safe zones of higher dimension—not "work-free" zones, but safe zones.

But don't think of yourself as being specially selected or superior to others who are working elsewhere. It is yours to do because it is in you to do; it is your job. Your group is simply the one appropriate for you. The same truth can and will be experienced through different forms.

(I grew up in a religious environment/tradition that pretty much figured that if you didn't think their way there was something wrong with your thinking. Most of us probably grew up that way. I finally got free of that, and joined a small group of people who meditated daily and studied religious texts from all over the world. We were all so proud that we had broken with tradition and found "the truth." As our group grew in number we took on rules and regulations, and began to develop an identity. We became sort of the Hindu equivalent to hardshell Baptists, changing our costumes but not our limitations.)

Strict identification with any one form, however conducive to the Spirit, is merely an extension of ego. We each have a role or purpose to fulfill, but one person's task is never more important than another's. You are judged by how you judge others. How you treat the ones who are asleep will be the measure of your own soul/salvation.

Everything is happening so fast right now that there is simply no time to spend in a specific place, at a particular altar, paying homage to a single method or teacher. Don't wait for someone else to do it for you or tell you how. Pursue your own ascension according to your own understanding and service. As you move through the cycles of prayer to meditation, to contemplation, to union, to one, you will be shown. You are all of these on the run, so to speak. All that you need is already present inside of you, waiting to be recognized. The altar is movable. The ascension is equal. You will experience it in whatever way you can accept it.

As individuals and groups focus on ascension, they should focus on recreating their lives as expressions of joy. As you do this, you shift everyone you come into contact with in your daily life, broadcasting the energy of joy to them and waking them up to that frequency. The mass ascension will occur when the majority of ascending humans on the planet are existing in a state of joy, and not until.

In this dimensional universe, free will is divine law. When the majority of you are living from joy, the planetary experience will have moved into a world of love and oneness. When the majority of you have given up the game of polarity because you have learned all you could, and have by your own choice moved into joy and oneness, the mass ascension will occur.

Until that time comes, and it will, the light-body progression will continue. The ascension will take as long as it takes. In the end, humanity as a collective decides the timing of this spectacular event. Free will cannot be tampered with, not even for good cause, not even to create the ascension.

So, be patient with the ascension. It means more of you coming here. More of you embodied. More of you remembering where you came from and what you are here to do. And as you bring that here, you lift everything into a higher expression by the mere fact that you connect inside and you become peace, and you become wisdom, and you become love. You assist everything in your experience, visibly and invisibly.

Perhaps the best way in which you can serve God, serve all mankind, serve the planet, and serve yourselves is to create your lives as expressions of joy. Be ruthless in evaluating your lives, and clear everything that does not bring you joy. Come into integrity. Let go of old emotions, old issues, even old relationships that are consuming the energy you could be feeling joy with. This path makes the ascension very simple; all that's required is for each individual to begin focusing on and taking responsibility for his own life. There are no victims here, and everyone is responsible for keeping his own cage clean.

—from the Journal, March/April, 1997

Brain Surgery

I believe it was Carl Jung who said that physical decay is the beginning of the "Great Work": spiritual transformation. Paracelsus wrote, "Decay is the beginning of all birth . . . midwife of great things . . . the deepest mystery and miracle that He/God has revealed to man." Indeed, people who have endured great physical trauma—war injuries, automobile accidents, surgery, even torture—do bear witness to this mystery with stories of light, angelic presences, and religious conversion. It would seem that physical pain cancels the claims of the world and the hold of ordinary consciousness, opening us up to other levels of thought and thinking. For certain, the ascension is being driven by an entirely new consciousness, by *other*world forces that threaten our comfort zones and challenge whatever paradigms we may be holding to.

That said, let's get personal.

My teacher had me pegged from the start: I am stubborn, slow to learn, and take everything personally. I woke up one morning with a headache so excruciating that I became convinced I had developed a brain tumor. I say this only half in jest; at the time, it was a genuine concern. In addition to the headaches, my vision was blurred, I couldn't think straight, couldn't walk straight, couldn't navigate my car without scaring the hell out of whomever might be riding with me. And I couldn't remember how to get into my computer. But for the headaches I would have thought it was early Alzheimer's.

And, of course, it was much too personally debilitating to be part of the ascension process. I knew that. I continued to know it even though I had a number of friends who were suddenly coming to me and describing similar symptoms. Three of them even went so far as to have an MRI (magnetic resonance imaging) done on their brain, just to see what was going on in there. Nothing was going on.

Good for them, I thought.

My own pain was different somehow, *more*, too *real* not to be happening. And I held to that thought, and my suffering, for a few more weeks, until finally the Brothers sat me down on my couch one afternoon and informed me that, yes, it was real, but no more or less so than anything else going on in the universe; that we were all experiencing the side effects of a cerebral surgery taking place at the etheric level, making way for the new brain system necessary for ascending into the reduced density of higher consciousness. That's what they told me, and within a few hours all my symptoms were gone. And stayed gone.

It was a mixed blessing. Of course I was glad to be healthy and alive. But I was embarrassed to tell my friends that I wasn't going to die after all.

And not long after, I was informed that a number of friends and acquaintances would indeed suffer brain tumors and strokes, all having to do with the ascension, the shift of consciousness into a higher octave of existence. It seems that whatever changes necessary for moving into the new day, Earth after the ascension, have to be made while in the body—while *alive*, in other words. Brains are being overhauled, nervous systems rewired. And those who are young enough, or strong enough, or, indeed, have consciousness enough to accept the changes, will stay in body and go on with their new lives, helping others to make similar transformations. Those who require too much change to integrate into this life, or are perhaps needed on the "other side," will be seeded with the new brain system, then drop the body and cross over. (The deepest parts of ourselves are also the oldest and most resistant to change, genetic predilections we carry around as karma.) You won't die. Not in any permanent sense. Consciousness simply is. Who you are never dies. You'll simply be brought back in the new day (reincarnated), with a new body and a new mind filled with new consciousness already up and running.

I have a friend whose father fit into this last category. Hospitalized with a massive stroke, he was distracted and confused at times, but did not seem to be in pain. Not so, his family. They watched him deteriorate daily, and suffered. His daughter wanted to know if he was all right in there, meaning inside of whatever was going on in his head during all this, inside the stroke. I offered, perhaps foolishly, to find out what I could, not really knowing what that meant or what might be involved.

What follows is not something I have ever done before or since. It is just something that seemed to grow out of the moment. I took his hand in mine, took a deep breath, and went "inside," surrendering myself to the moment and the situation, asking to be of service, asking to be protected, asking to be shown. The Brothers pretty much did the rest.

Suddenly I was inside of his head, looking out from his eyes. I can't say that I "felt" everything he was feeling exactly, but I was permitted to *observe* myself experiencing it. We seemed to share a common space, and for the next four harrowing and bizarre hours I manifested all the symptoms of a stroke. At first I felt trapped, panicky, afraid of losing my mind before my body had a chance to decide if it wanted to quit or recover. Unable to get free, get out, find sympathy or a cure outside myself, I couldn't think, I couldn't talk, I couldn't feed myself. I couldn't walk without stumbling, and eventually had to be driven home.

Isolation and stillness were all I had. And that created a sort of walled space around me, intensifying and incubating a curative process broiling inside myself. It was not unlike a sweat lodge. Only more so. And with no exit. But my mind was not distracted by movement and so turned back on itself in an *inward* spiral, like a whirlpool, drifting into an altered state of twilight sleep to be informed by the healing gods and goddesses, the Brothers. There were lightbeings everywhere.

The lightbeings seemed to be performing some sort of surgery on my brain (his brain? our brain?), an operation that made laser surgery seem primitive, actually rerouting certain circuitry, making connections where there had previously been none. I was amazed. I felt glorified. There was even a part of me that was assisting in what was going on. And the only time I felt discomfort was when I tried to communicate with some one of my family in the room. I couldn't make them understand that, other than the frustration of not being able to tell them about it, I felt fine. The only misery was the misery on everyone's face as they tried to get me to perform the same old tricks they were accustomed to seeing. They were so locked into their own mindset of how I used to be that they couldn't see me as I was/am now. Newly born. In the Spirit. I had one foot on this side of the veil and one foot on the other. The only pain was from trying to make sense of *That* to family and friends, doctors and nurses who were cognizant only of *this. This.* I cried, but it was more from frustration than pain, and certainly not from a sense of loss.

Of course, trying to do things, mundane things, like eat, read, emit, wipe my own nose, all that, made me irritable, even inconsolable when I couldn't. And I'm sure there were subtleties of the illness that I was not made to suffer, but all in all my friend's father was not having a bad time in there. And the deeper part of him understood and appreciated the work being done on his behalf.

Over the next several weeks I watched this same process repeated again and again, his body changing, losing weight, luster, and vitality, while assuming an ethereal tenor. More than a state of being, his illness became a process of transformation, his spiritual path and practice. I came to realize that deep inside any illness is a dissolving process that melts walls and rigidities, opening us up to the full chaos and mystery of life. While these processes are often described as stages, they do not occur in any particular sequence; we slip in and out of them, back and forth, spending more time in some than others, according to our own inclinations and the requirements of our souls. There are moments of great fear, and times of absolute euphoria. In reality there are no stages, only the incessant changes of the mind. In his early days in the hospital, the more he complained about his situation, the less sympathetic were the people around him; his despair seemed to short-circuit their capacities for attention and compassion. However, after a particularly difficult night of self-confrontation, it was as though he decided to keep the despair to himself; that, or he just decided not to entertain it anymore—and a curious shift occurred.

Sometime in the night, I heard him muttering under his breath, over and over, almost like a chant; "I am not who I am anymore. I am not who I am anymore. I am not who I am anymore." And from that day on, even though his body continued to deteriorate, his spirit seemed to get larger, brighter, infused with a soft gold light. I'm sure he felt scared and frustrated on occasions, but he had a new way about him, a new power; his soul, like a muscle, got stronger with each night he survived. I watched his agitation turn to clarity, his suffering turn to grace. After that night I don't believe he ever spoke again. But he never stopped smiling. He knew something we didn't, and he wasn't about to diminish it by talking about it.

The work was done. His new cerebral system was wired and in place, new consciousness seeded.

One night when he was alone in the room and no one was looking, he quietly and peacefully slipped away.

—from the Journal, April of 1998

FROM GRIEF TO GRACE, THE CLEANSING PROCESS

This morning I woke up feeling that something was very wrong. I couldn't pinpoint what, only a sense of agitation, as if something terrible were about to happen. I put on my clothes and walked outside.

The sky was high and clear. One of those perfect fall days that happen too often in Oklahoma. Everything seemed to be in place. Nothing going on. But it was difficult to breathe, or at least catch a deep breath. At first I felt anxious, but that soon gave way to an overwhelming sense of grief and grieving. For what or for whom I had no idea, but I felt devastated.

I undressed and went back to bed.

A short time later I got up again.

Then back to bed. Up and down, up and down, for hours. All with a deep sense of grieving and loss. Finally I moved onto the couch and just sat there looking at nothing. Somewhere someone was dying and I was desperate to know who, in what way I was connected.

Most of my family are gone. I have a daughter in Texas and a cousin in Arkansas, but it didn't seem to have anything to do with them; intuitively I *felt* like they were all right. This was more personal even than that, closer to home. The obvious occurred to me, that I might be the one dying (more accurate than I realized, but in ways less terminal than I was yet to understand). I had no pains or physical symptoms other than feeling heavy and depressed. And I was too full of my own discomfort to go "inside" and ask for assistance.

So the Brothers intervened on my behalf. Actually, I think I said something like, *Jesus H. Christ, what's going on here*! and they took that to be a plea for help. I was more exasperated than anything, but they responded. They said that it had to do with the transformation of my self. In keeping with the ascension, my entire cellular structure was being overhauled, and part of it would probably have to die off; in other words, I was losing cellular memory and grieving the loss of it. That's what I was told. I was grieving the loss of the old self that no longer served my new purpose, and the loss was so deep and profound that it triggered the grieving process in me. A part of me *was* dying, and the part of me that remained was grieving the loss of it.

Of course, I was only interested in immediate personal relief.

Don't ignore the grief, they said. Don't set it aside or suppress it. This is an emotional clearing and, as with all emotions, you should totally embrace the *energy* of it. But do so without judgment, especially *self*-judgment. Emotions may vary in both intensity and vibration, but it is always your thoughts about those emotions that give them their charge. (For example: anger is a positive charge, depression is a negative charge—same energy coming from the same place, different only in electrical charge. And it is your judgment that makes the determination.) To transmute your anger or fear into *raw energy*, simply don't judge it. Don't use the intellect to judge your thoughts or emotions. Releasing judgment means setting your thoughts aside and trusting your feelings. As soon as you do that, the energy changes. Not the intensity of it, but the *intent*. Feel the energy without giving in to its original surge; channel the energy in a different direction.

Feeling is a combination of emotion and thought. When you feel your emotions, when you are releasing something, stay completely present with the feeling or emotion you are experiencing. In this case, allow yourself to feel the grieving, but without trying to pin it on anything or identifying with it. It's not necessary to know where it's coming from. Who may or may not be at fault is not the issue. Indeed, as part of the ascension process, these things are occurring on a planetary level. They are happening in your fields as they are occurring in many fields of many beings all simultaneously. So, don't try to figure out what is causing the feeling. Instead, focus on how it feels and where it seems to be located in your body. And allow it to be. Allow it to move around. Of course, don't allow yourself the luxury of falling into it so completely that you lose yourself in it. In that moment, decide to be present fully in the emotion, in the feeling, and simply *observe* yourself experiencing it.

Grief, fear, anger, anxiety, those are all just labels for identifying an energy that is moving through your body of consciousness. *Don't identify with the labels.* Don't react to them; reacting simply puts them back into your pattern to deal with again later. Instead, choose to observe them without judgment, and then ride them out, complete the clearing, and be done with it. That way there is no residue left over, nothing left hanging out in your energy fields.

Then I was given a mental exercise for transmuting the energy: When you feel that energy rise, I was told, whether it is in your chest, your belly, or your throat, keep lifting it up. Lift it with your breath. What comes into you as, say, anger or fear, changes as you move it up from the belly, through the heart, past the intellect, passing through a mild state of bliss resonating from the crown chakra. Keep moving it with your breath, right on up and out through the top of your head. Feel it. Allow yourself to feel it in your entire being. But keep moving it on up and into spirit. Spirit will know what to do with it. Spirit will show you how to be in it without being of it, how to be one with it, and be above it, all at the same time.

So I embraced my grieving, and continued to suffer for another day and a half. (Perhaps the most difficult paradox we are asked to entertain is that of trusting the pain as well as the light, to allow the emotion, grief in this case, to penetrate while keeping one's heart open to the perfection of the universe.) I was miserable, not fit for human consumption. But I no longer felt like I was, me personally, under attack by the universe. I grieved, but the grieving no longer felt terminal or personal. And I was aware the very minute it let up. I felt like my soul had undergone a high colonic. I was as clean and clear and light as I had been for weeks, months even. Ready for the next thing.

END OF KARMA/BIRTH OF COMPASSION

At the same time the above was going on, the Brothers were quick to point out that not all of my grieving was the result of personal/individual cleansing. As part of the ascension, the entire planetary consciousness was going through the same process, and I was in some way attuned to that. (The earthquakes in Turkey were going on; hurricanes were battering the East Coast; the entire planet was being stressed and stretched to the max.) Then I was made to recall something that had occurred four years earlier.

This next is a bit of a stretch even for me. Without watering it down or pumping it up, I'm just going to describe my experience of it as accurately as I can. Its occasion is not that widespread, occurring primarily to those lightbeings who have come here to assist in the ascension/transformation process. My guess is, if you've read this far, then it probably applies to you.

In the spring of 1995, I was living in a cabin on a private lake thirty minutes from Oklahoma

City. For over a year I'd been meeting with a hand-ful of friends—doctors, therapists, healers of all kinds—gathered together to meditate and share experiences of our transformation into the "new day," whatever that meant. None of us were quite sure, but it felt right. We were oriented toward service to spirit, *unconditional* service, as best we could, and to the extent we understood what that meant.

In February, a number of our group began to experience an unidentifiable grief, which turned to mourning. No explanation for it. Nothing in anyone's life to warrant such a response. Feeling raw and vulnerable, it was as puzzling as it was depressing. Then three of us began having dreams of carnage, bloody dismemberment everywhere. More disturbing was the hangover it left us with, the details lingering around all day and into the evening. The knee-jerk reaction was to think of it as being karmically linked to us personally; that we were in some way responsible for whatever was going on, or about to happen.

In meditation, we were all asking to be informed in some deep, fully conscious place beyond the ocean of mind. But not until we were reminded of the words and urgings of our teacher did we get some relief. My teacher's constant mes-sage was not to take anything, especially your own life, personally. That goes for dreams, emotions, any imaginings, as well as the so-called "real stuff" of your lives; don't take them personally. Observe what is going on, acknowledge what is going on, don't deny anything that is happening; serve the moment that is put before you, but don't tangle yourself in it.

At the same time, we began to feel some collective purpose related to what we were experiencing, a growing suspicion that we were serving some larger, albeit unidentified, cause. But when we went inside and asked for clarity, we were shut down. Told, in no uncertain terms, that we did not need to know the details at that time, that knowing too much too early would hinder our ability not only to serve, but to function day to day. Do the work, we were told. Trust your life. And don't worry about if or when. A giant leap of faith was required.

Meanwhile, the dreams didn't stop. The mourning didn't stop. We were each of us subject to break into tears without warning. The temptation was to think we had collectively decided to have a nervous breakdown. The experience became one of learning how to observe one's own life without taking it personally; personally, it made no sense anyway. As we grew better at relating to it in that way, it began to feel more like a cleansing than a burden. There were nights when I felt like my entire soul was being scoured, skewered, and cleansed in a single act. But I had to let go of how I thought about what was going on, whatever judgment I might have. Something wonderful and devastating was taking place, and I felt torn open and glorified in the same instant; not to mention mystified.

Our wildest imaginings could not have prepared us for what happened next.

On April 19, 1995, the Alfred P. Murrah building in downtown Oklahoma City was bombed, resulting in the loss of one hundred and sixty eight lives. I'll not attempt to reproduce the details here.

You've seen and read about it at length. Nothing I could say would add to what has already been said.

Members of our group went to work immediately.

We had already done the grieving and the mourning. Without knowing it, we had been rehearsing this moment for weeks and months. As a group of professional healers, our skills were immediately useful. What followed were days and weeks of long hours, digging through the rubble, and assisting those who were involved in the rescue effort. All of it done in an environment that you would expect to be exhausting and overwhelmingly depressing. But that was not the case, at least not where our group was concerned.

From the start, we were aware of something going on behind and beyond the scenes. Not something political or mundane as that; certainly not something to be judged or argued; not something to ask yourself why it happened or what should be done about it; something more than even the personal devastation reverberating through everyone's life. From the moment we arrived on the scene, we were aware of what I can only describe as this divine, motherly presence hovering above the place, and a host of lightbeings quietly circulating among the stunned crowd. I watched—*felt*—the miracle take place; watched as the lightbeings inhabited individual people and performed acts of heroism; watched as the Divine Mother pulled the suffering up into her bosom. Nothing changed. The suffering would not be removed, nor the lives returned. But there it was. Their grief became her grief, their sorrow her own. And though they grieved not one bit less for it, their lives were made larger, with room enough for her heart, her wisdom, and her compassion. And each of us bore the sorrow better.

Our group felt blessed by the whole ordeal. Not without sympathy for the victims and their families, we were, nevertheless, aware of a larger, deeper purpose being served. It was not something we cognized immediately and said, "Oh, of course, that's what it is." That would come much later. But it was something we felt immediately. A feeling that, at the time, went beyond words or anyone's ability to share. Indeed, my present difficulty is in finding words to explain how, in the midst of all that suffering, there was a pocket of people who felt absolutely glorified. We felt blessed and grateful to witness the ringing down of the karmic day, and the birth of the compassionate heart in America—all in a single act in a single moment.

Everything we know and have been informed by since tells us that the karmic day must come to an end before we can go on to the next dimension, the next octave of consciousness, Earth in the new day. The people who died in the bombing sacrificed their lives to that end. And with the clearing of that huge block of karma (karma, incidentally, owing to the entire country), the *purpose* of karma and reincarnation were revealed: to learn compassion and make a permanent space in our heart for it. That's all. That's enough. It need serve no other purpose. And suddenly we knew all that. We didn't know what it was that we knew, or how we knew it, but something in our *feeling nature* understood. And it made our work over the next several days easier, our task, then and now, lighter.

That's not to say we didn't suffer like everyone else, but our suffering was buoyed by grace. In the midst of the most awful feelings you could ever imagine, we felt glorified, lifted right up into what could only be described as the heart of something Motherly. We cried. We all cried, with a sorrow informed by grace.

I don't mean to suggest that we were the only people who felt or experienced this event in a similar way. I'm sure there were others. But it was not something you could readily share with your co-workers on the scene; not everyone would understand. Fortunately, we had each other.

It was the most dramatic example I've yet experienced of what it means to "process for the collective," and why it is absolutely imperative that you not take anything personally. A wonderfully difficult time. "Difficult," if, as a lightbeing, you identify too closely with the density level you have come to serve; "wonderful," if you can just remember who you are, where you came from, and what exactly you came here to do in the first place.

Amazing things are afoot in the universe. Don't underestimate your role in it. This planet reflects what is happening to each of us individually. We are all connected. I am, *You* is, we all are, more than previously imagined, certainly more than the human condition. And service is our reason for being here.

—from the Journal, September, 1999

THE GOD WITHIN

This next may seem contradictory in the face of what you've read so far, perhaps more so in light of what is to follow. But I no longer think of the incident that marked the beginning of this book as channeling; at least not from some external source. Nor are any subsequent incidents channeled. I am not being dictated to by beings that are out of body, though it might seem so on occasions. Instead, I am being made to connect with some deep projection of my self, some inner voice, call it the higher self, call it the divine self, the deep self, whatever; this is about learning to listen to the *spirit within* rather than any external authority. That spirit isn't out to trick you or terrify you; quite the opposite. Its purpose is to guide and inform. In doing so, it will appear to you in a way that you are best able to accept and blend with it. It may change costumes from time to time; it may even alter an occasional fact, but it never lies.

I call that spirit, the *god within*, and while it may not be all-knowing, it certainly has a greater perspective than my personality self could ever imagine on its own.

The god within is an element of the universal hologram that makes possible an intimate relationship with the Creator/Mother/Father/God of us all. It makes personal experience of the divinity a reality. Without knowledge of the god within, you may experience the Spirit of God, but you will never know its source within yourself. In order to know God at this level, you must be prepared to surrender your ordinary mind for the extraordinary; give up all belief systems and stop looking for something or someone "out there" to save you. There is nothing out there but illusion, projections of self/ego, gods of many faces—true gods, perhaps, but with limited truth. To fully experience the one Creator/God, you must be willing to confront, do battle with, and embrace the god within. Of course, when your desire to know the God within is strong enough and sincere enough, you are first made to confront all your illusions of what you think God is by looking at everything God is not. Everything in your life that detracts from the experience of knowing the god within will be attracted to you, and will fail.

Your life may fail you. The human world you live in may break down and stop working in ways you think it should. You may experience abandonment and betrayal; neither of which is intended to hurt you in any ultimate sense, but to bring you into harmony with your deep Self. In order to know the god within, you must first know what it is to be alone and separated: from family, friends, lovers, jobs, any and every security you may think you have; there are no boundaries, no limits to the inconvenience your divine Self may put you through, until you feel temporarily disconnected from the world of cause and effect. You may feel depression and fatigue; you may manifest illness . . . whatever it takes to break your death grip on the material world and cause you, for one brief moment, to doubt the world you think you know.

In that moment, your spirit will begin to detach from the physical/material life you have been living. Walls may seem to move, buildings, even whole cities will seem to be made of cardboard. You may not be able to locate your own feelings, how you feel about anything. You will stop trusting the very things in your life that have brought you here, suffering the breakdown of the very concepts that have previously supported you. You must enter yourself alone, separate and separated, before you can then be put back together and made whole.

And the only way out of the above named shit and desperation is to turn to your own intuitive guidance, your god within.

In that instant in which you begin to cooperate with God, you realize that God never really needed your cooperation in the first place. You cannot make a wrong choice. You cannot choose the wrong life or the wrong occupation. Your family, friends, and lovers are perfect; they are, at least to this moment, exactly who you need. You are always doing exactly what God intends for you to be doing. Frustration and anger ensues only when you think you should be living your life any other way. The god within you brought you here. If you would rather be someone else, somewhere else, you are always free to choose and choose again, but even your decision to choose differently is guided by your god within.

Each of you is a perfect expression of God's intent. You have within you the capacity to make mistakes but not to fail. Failure is an illusion of those who serve a god of fear, a god whose love is contingent and incomplete.

—from the Journal entry, April 25-May 8, 1996
revisited in October of 1999

MANDALA

Having come this far, having undergone an intense three years, or more, of transformation in which my entire belief system had been shattered, I thought nothing else could surprise me. Not true. In fact, this next series of events threatened to finally push me right over the edge of . . . *what*? I'm not sure I know.

Understand, I am part of a small group of "recovering psychics," professional people—doctors, attorneys, teachers—who have been plagued and gifted by psychic experiences most of their lives. We number Baptists, Buddhists, Presbyterians, at least one qualified atheist, and a couple of recovering Catholics. Some of us had a common teacher and met nearly twenty years ago; some of us are new to each other. All seem to mirror, in some way or another, the new age that is transforming the planet daily, hourly, minute to minute. For three or four years we have been getting together on a weekly basis to meditate, share wonders and horror stories, and generally support one another's personal mutation into the new day. It is an informal group, unified by one thing:

an insatiable curiosity about the higher dimensions. We have no bylaws and few expectations of one another. Our collective agenda is simply to serve Spirit.

However, there is no end to the caprice Spirit is willing to perform in order to get your attention and teach you the next step along the path, whatever that next step might be. In fact, there is a running joke among our group: *Are you ready for the "next thing?"* And of course, no one is.

But we are willing.

In all honesty, I can't say that I ever actually look forward to taking the next step, but I have come to expect and anticipate it, and I am always grateful for the results.

For several weeks I had been suffering through one of those long, flat, boring spaces that sometimes occur between interventions of Spirit. I needed a "hit," some minor miracle to let me know I had not been forgotten. I am such a Spirit-junky that I can actually go through withdrawal symptoms when I think I'm without it. Of course I'm not; no one ever is. But I'd managed to work myself into a lingering depression.

Unable to meditate for days, I lay down on my couch one afternoon and just gave up to wallowing in my condition without trying to escape or figure a way out. Screw it, I thought. This is where I am, this is where I'll stay. I dare you. I dare anyone, God, or anything to pull me out of this whatever-it-is.

And that's when the "next thing" happened.

Now, understand something: my studies, my work, have never been conducted rationally, but have to some extent been arrived at intuitively through certain coincidences, so called. Any answers usually come in the form of parables or puzzles or geometrical drawings, word doodads, something which ends up pointing me in the direction of a deeper understanding of the mystery or dysfunctional state I seem to be entertaining at the time. In addition, I have a habit of reading six or eight books, more or less simultaneously, by leaving them open and lying around my apartment, open to key pages or passages perhaps, but with no particular theme or continuity. In an evening's work I might move from reading Mark Twain's *Letters from the Earth*, to a book on astrology or astronomy, Hindu mythology, the dreams of Carl Jung, or the life and times of Larry Flint. It is a cross-disciplined approach comparing not only points of view but differences of language as well. Add to that list a dissertation on sacred geometry, and you have some idea what sort of flux my mind was in that day. Or maybe you don't.

But what happened next was extraordinary.

First let me say that there are no hidden metaphors here. This is the way it happened. This is the way it felt, as clearly as I can recall. And it started with all the open-paged passages from the books suddenly coalescing into a complete whole. Lying there on the couch, in my underwear, in the middle of the afternoon, an entirely new "on board" experience was about to take place.

Open-eyed and fully awake, a voice from deep inside myself told me to get up off my ass and "*Go to the window.*" I did, like an automaton, without thinking about it, without questioning where that voice might be coming from, and with no concern for the laws of gravity or time, I went to the window and opened the blinds. I stared up into a huge blue hole in an otherwise cloudy sky. In the center of this clear blue hole, and directly overhead, was a giant spinning mandala—it must have been a half mile in diameter. A mandala, I thought?

Then I had a moment of panic, wondering if perhaps this could be the end of something: my life? The world as I had come to know it? Battling against an immediate fear response, I tried to settle myself, or center myself, at least be calm while the next thing happened, whatever the next thing was. I tried to remember my own mantra and couldn't; I tried to recite the Lord's Prayer and couldn't do that. If this was to be my last moments, I wanted to be doing something, *anything* to help my cause. Then the words *Om Mani Padme Hum* began to resonate in my mind's ear, and I began to repeat them over and over.

Now I can't remember ever having used those words before, or having given them much thought. They are the Sanskrit words of a widely used Indian mantra. I knew that, but I had no idea what they meant. I have since learned that translated they mean: *"May the jewel of the lotus descend into your heart"*—a call to the opening of the heart of compassion. At the time, however, I had no clues as to what they meant or why they would be echoing out of my head, my heart, and my mouth. I was chanting them, and then I realized that they were not so much coming *out* of me as they were passing *through* me, resonating from the mandala overhead. Indeed, they caused my whole body to vibrate.

Wherever they came from, they had a calming effect, loving, safe. I felt suddenly at peace. This was the end of something or the beginning of something, and it didn't much matter.

Now all of this took just seconds, but in my heightened state of consciousness everything was moving in ultra slow motion. I was now in the middle of my own front yard, still in my underwear, looking up into this giant mandala which began to look very much like the spacecraft I'd seen three years ago—*exactly* three years ago according to my journal. There were rows and rows of lights, wheels of lights actually, wheels inside of wheels, each spinning at a different speed and in opposite directions. At the center of all this was some sort of geometric light construct having to do with sixth dimensional physics, I was told, two star-tetrahedrons, looking somewhat like interlocking pyramids or a six-pointed star, intertwined and appearing to spin counter to one another. The wheels of lights were connected, by twelve spokes, to the geometric construction in the center.

In that instant, I perceived that the laws of multidimensional travel were contained, in their entirety, in the geometrical proportions of this mandala with the two intertwined star-tetrahedrons at its center. More than that, the star-tetrahedrons represented a sort of mystic crystal in whose planes of refraction all the laws of the universe were perfectly reflected. In other words, they held the memory of the entire universe.

I knew that. Don't ask me *why* I knew it, or *how* I knew it, or what exactly it all meant. I just knew it. And the implications were greater than I could begin to imagine. (I would discover later that the twelve spokes represented twelve DNA strands that are starting to recode, as well as twelve regions in the universe linked to us through extra-terrestrial mythologies of human creation, e.g., Pleiades, Orion, Lyra/Vega, Andromeda, Arcturus, Zeta Riticulum, Sirius.)

Meanwhile, I was still in my front yard, still in my underwear, looking up into a clear blue hole in an otherwise dark sky. Cars were driving up and down the street. My neighbor was mowing his lawn. He waved and nodded in my direction, but he did not look up, and he did not stop his mow-ing. Whatever was going on, I was alone in it. (Later I would learn that They, the Brothers, are able to alter the brain frequency of individuals, making phenomena visible to some and not to others. I'm not sure whose brain waves had been altered, mine or my neighbors, but there it is.) When I looked back at the sky, the clouds had rolled together, the mandala had disappeared, and it was beginning to rain.

I was alone, sort of. Suddenly *You* was back. Remember *You*? from the early pages of this what-ever-it-is. I hadn't seen *You* since we were both teleported onto the lightship and *You* chose to stay on board.

You was back and it was like meeting up with a friend/lover/mate after a long absence. *You* was there to lead me back inside the house, telling me that I couldn't continue to stand in the front yard, in the rain, in broad daylight, in my underwear. *You* also told me that we were onboard again; that we had been onboard for quite some time. Onboard has been refurnished to look exactly like your living room, says *You*. And I don't say any-thing. Words fail me.

I was restless and wired that night, somewhat euphoric but unfocused. My mindscreen was so full that I couldn't separate one thing from another. And nothing looked familiar. When I did sleep I seemed to be in some sort of class conducted in a language foreign to me. Coming awake, I heard Greek-sounding words deep inside me. Of course, I don't speak Greek, so I can't be sure. Shortly after daybreak I got up and moved to the couch. What followed, I have no explanation for, no proof, nothing convincing except my own intuitive sense of it. I'm just going to tell you what was conveyed to me in a series of thought-forms that continued unabated for the next three days. If this account seems anomalous and inconsistent, attribute that to my attempts to, once more, talk about something I know nothing about. In measuring its veracity, I encourage you to keep an open mind but to use your own discretion, listen to your own inner guidance.

My First Four Billion Years

This was not a bedroom scene, no sleeping or dreaming is involved. Lying on my couch, fully awake, my eyes wide open, I began to remember things I could not possibly have known before, and which I do not recall ever having read.

Four billion years ago, it seems, the human species was a root race scattered throughout the universe and seemed to have no real home galaxy or planet of its own. They were always the working class, almost slave labor. For whatever reason, it was determined that they would be the subject of what would thereafter be referred to simply as the "noble experiment." As such, the human species was "harvested" (not my word) from all over the universe and brought to Andromeda (I'm not sure if that's the Andromeda Galaxy or the sun system in our own galaxy; perhaps I am supposed to know, but I don't). We were there to attend pre-Earth school alongside a race of lightbeings who had volunteered to participate in the experiment. We all came together on Andromeda and began our schooling.

On Andromeda we went through a long orientation. I can't really say how long since, outside of the third dimension, time has a way of expanding or collapsing to accommodate the situation. The rest of the universe is in sort of all-time-now; it schedules *events* but doesn't really keep time. For that same reason, I'm not really sure if "four billion years" means four billion years, either. I'm simply telling you what I was told.

Anyway, each lightbeing was assigned a group or family of humans to go through the experiment with. We began our training by putting humans on and taking them off, like costumes or space suits we had to get used to. Each day we were required to put at least one human on and wear it all day; not until we went to sleep at night could we take it off. I remember how unnatural, even suffocating, the human suits were at first, with buttons and knobs and strange appendages I had no use for at the time. We drafted the first plans for a personal ego-body to take care of the human suits while on planet Earth, but no one was willing to try one on yet.

A primary element of the experiment was the loss of memory it required. A loss of memory was necessary in order to be totally immersed in the experiment as a "local." We had to be convinced and convincing in every detail. In order to do this, a large part of our genetic memory would need to be erased, to make it authentic. We had to really appear to be locals; we had to *believe* we were humans. I remember sitting in class with a lot of other beings from around the universe, all of us laughing at the very idea of giving up our memory, thinking we really were our costumes. It looked interesting, even fun. Being gods, being there, then, none of us could have imagined how total that loss of memory would be; or the consequences.

After our orientation and schooling on Andromeda, we were transported to the star system Lyra/Vega deep in the center of this galaxy, the Milky Way. We were eleventh density/dimension beings, star beings, not quite human yet, but third density was under construction and planet Earth was being seeded with terra firma in preparation for our arrival. From Lyra we broke up into smaller groups and went to different parts of the galaxy for more training. Some went to Sirius to learn sixth dimensional physics—sacred geometry, light engineering, all that. Some went to the Pleiades to be fitted for a "feeling nature"—passion at one end of the spectrum, the compassionate heart at the other. We tried on our emotional bodies for the first time. Briefly. It was at once exhilarating and maddening. The only thing that made that experience tolerable was the fact that we still had our memory intact. We rethought and redesigned the personality-ego again. We visited the Universal Library at Alcyone in the Pleiades, even helped build a new wing on the Library dedicated solely to tracking the progress of our experiment throughout the universe. We laughed, again, at the prospect of building a library and an elaborate set of records in a place that we would soon not remember how to find or even that it existed.

We eventually came back together again at Arcturus, to be retooled and re-intentioned. Our jobs were made more specific. No two of us would have the exact same job. Everyone was necessary. No one could be lost on this mission. If one got lost, left behind, or injured in some debilitating way, we were all responsible for them. We were still in *all*-time, but we built a chamber dedicated to linear-time and experimented with the effects of memory loss. For the first time since our recruitment and training began, Andromeda seemed like a long way off; some of us could barely remember it.

Are you with me so far? We've gotten through the easy part.

Leaving Arcturus and moving into this solar system—for most of us Venus was our last stop before arriving on planet Earth—our mission was taken out of the classroom and made more specific, more personal. Our task was to somehow create a new species, a new planetary being, with interdimensional capabilities; in other words, the ability to live and operate *consciously* on *all* dimensions simultaneously. As progenitors of this new species, we are genetically related to at least twenty-two different extraterrestrial species and endowed with Spirit. More than that, we have *free will*.

More than any other species, it seems, we do have free will. The gods and goddesses are confined to their own realm; angels are confined to their own realm; all beings from inner space and outer space, including the Brothers, are confined to their own realm. We alone are not confined; at least, not in any ultimate sense. All "realms" exist inside of us. As forerunners to a divinely human species, the unique aspect of the One that we most represent is free will. It is God's gift to us for participating in the noble experiment. God gave us free will and bound Itself to this. Choose what you will, there are no mistakes. Even those choices that seem to be in error, God finds complete and satisfying.

We are living in wonderfully volatile times in which anything can and will happen, depending on our intent and the sincerity of our desires/efforts. Free will is a divine right of this dimensional universe; we are free to create the universe of our dreams and imaginings, limited only by our willingness to accept responsibility for our being, our soul, and the living of its life/lives. The more responsibility we accept, the more free will we are allowed.

The human species was chosen to be the inheritors of this experiment, lab rats made into *what*? Gods? At least. More than gods, perhaps. So the human species was harvested from all over the universe. Prior to that they were not born but *grown* and cultivated as a slave race, the laboring community of the universe. As such, they had limited consciousness, no free will, and no soul as we/you understand it. All of these things had to be added to the human DNA, one element at a time, gradually over a four billion year period (one day in the life of God, I'm told).

First, consciousness had to be added, and with it, free will; these two elements work together: enough consciousness is necessary to know that there are choices, and enough free will is needed to make them; they had to learn to make choices—not right choices over wrong choices, but *any* choice; then they had to learn that each choice has its consequences. In other words, man is given free will before he is given wisdom, so he is destined to make mistakes, and learn from them.

Eventually, the "feeling nature" was added, the emotional body was built, the compassionate heart was ignited, and soul infusion took place.

Soul Infusion: When Higher Mind is made to balance and blend with the Compassionate Heart, soul is generated and infused into a living body. Spirit comes alive. This is true throughout the universe. The task or experiment we have undertaken is the infusion of soul into an entire species, thereby creating an entirely *new* species—the planetary-Christed-child-being with inter-dimensional consciousness enough not only to *know* the path, but to *walk* the path, to *be* it. "Knowing" the path may be accomplished through higher mind. But to be able to walk it requires heart as well. And soul infusion makes that possible. It is the object of all this: not simply to ascend into spirit or move from one dimension to another, but to understand that soul infusion is not only the means of ascension, but the point of it. Living, being *alive*, requires that a physical body be endowed with consciousness. *Soul infusion is an absolute prerequisite to* living *in the Spirit.*

We, as a race of lightbeings living in the Spirit, fully conscious and infused with soul, volunteered to inhabit the entire human species in order to walk them through the process; to influence, but not manipulate their choices; to act as midwife to their birth into the celestial realms, the Universe of Spirit. And that is why so much is made of bringing the heart and mind into a perfect balance; each time that balance occurs we are graced by the presence of Higher Mind and the Compassionate Heart, a deeper awareness of soul takes place, and more soul is infused into the body of the human consciousness.

The conclusion of the noble experiment will be the creation of an entirely new planetary being.

What we are beginning to remember finally, is the *totality* of our Soul, the completeness of it. The only reason we are ever out of sorts—out of "integrity"—is because we have forgotten some element of our soul; we have not "sinned," we have just forgotten. And it is in the process of our *remembering* that consciousness and soul are instilled into our human charges, the individual human species.

It is of interest to note that during the entire three days of these transmissions, I ate very little, slept in fits and spurts, the phone didn't ring once, and not a soul (incarnate) came to my door. While I am something of a city hermit, I do have a network of friends and acquaintances that come by or call daily. But for three days there was nothing. Just me and *You.*

Somewhere in the middle of the third day, however, enough space opened up in the transmissions for me to voice some concerns. Actually, I didn't really voice anything. As in the past, all I had to do was think it, and they answered what they deemed relevant.

Most of all, I just wanted to know why I was suddenly remembering all this now, why is it necessary to remember it at all, and why are there days in which it feels more like a punishment than a blessing? To what purpose is all this? And, again, just *who* are you?

They told me that we, the race of lightbeings who volunteered to assist the human species, have merged and blended with our human counterparts in order to fully understand, appreciate, and have compassion for their condition. This descent into human consciousness has been mislabeled as the

171

"fall from grace," and indeed, it is a separation from grace. But it was not a mistake, nor is it punishment for having lived a life of sin and foolish choices, unless *service* to the Divine is a foolish choice. Descending into the human species was a courageous and unselfish act of service motivated by compassion.

Of course you are always subject to the laws of the place and dimension you have chosen to serve. We understood that, in the abstract. But until we had seen it from the human perspective we did not know how limiting those laws could be, how oppressive and painful are the effect of those laws on those of us who are equal to the universe and beyond any law of limitation.

We came to serve the human species in a third density world, and we are subject to all the laws of that world. We have taken the human species on, in, and about ourselves to the point of identifying with them totally. In fact, not until we began to believe we were human did our part of the experiment actually take effect. As we reach critical mass, and right on schedule, we are triggered to begin to remember.

That's where we are now, at different stages of our remembering; remembering *who* we are, *what* we are, *where* we came from, and, ultimately, *why* we are doing all this. Soul is the recorded memory of who and what we are in the universe. Our job is simply to remember the *totality* of our soul, that we are part and parcel of the entire universe. As the deeper part of our Self remembers another aspect of its soul, the human ego responds to that with an Aha!, an experience of enlightenment. Enlightenment and soul are different expressions of the same event. *And it is in the process of our remembering that the human species wakes up.*

We are remembering, the human inside each of us is waking up. *Resonant evolution*: Knowing who you are, and emanating who you are, causes the evolution of everything in your environment to accelerate, and it causes the human residing inside each of you to wake up. And with each waking, each quickening, more light is let in; more consciousness is let in, more compassion. The result is that more soul is infused into the human species and with it, the attendant Spirit.

At the soul level, you incarnate not only in other dimensions, but on other planets in other systems. As you enter the light, your frequency increases until you vibrate in a new expression, or dimension, of who you are. You are not related to the Pleiadians, and the Sirians, and the Arcturians: you *are* them. You are not *like* the Brothers, you *are* the Brothers; not similar to, but different aspects of the same one Being.

As part of a family or soul group larger than you can imagine, each of you carries a different part of a light project you have come here to accomplish. To do that, all you have to do is reflect and resonate your perfect lineage. It is a lineage that comes from star systems you are beginning to remember, star systems that resonate in the diamond frequency spinning at the speed of thought, yet maintaining the physical body. This is your lineage and your destiny carried in your DNA as memories, memories of these star systems as well as of pre-Atlantean Egypt that existed before the free-will mutation of your genetic codings—that latter being the aspect of your agreement that you obviously don't remember. It is part of your soul contract, however, necessary for the successful completion of your assignment on planet Earth.

Some of you whose consciousness has been raised may understand what's going on, but many do not. It is a time of confusion and those who know teach those who don't. Many of you will try to deny what is taking place because your belief system is just not big enough to accommodate what is going on. But no soul who has ever lived here will miss out.

Memory of your lightbody is returning to you. Your urge to remember is a real thing in your body, as strong as any sexual urge you have ever had. It will become your highest aspiration.

In the meantime, think of this as a banquet of opportunity, and everyone who is anyone is here: Mother, Father, God, and all the little gods, your galactic brothers and sisters. If you can imagine them, they're here, hanging out inter-dimensionally, watching and observing, wondering when does the party start; some are even making side bets on what might happen next and just what you will/might turn into. In a universe of free will, there are no guarantees. You are witnessing the unfoldment of a grand will, the Divine Will, as it blends with your own free will to co-create the ascension.

And just *who* are we? you ask. That's the key to recovering your memory, remembering that there is only one of us here; that only one of us has ever been here. And it's *you*. (Is there an echo in here, or have we heard all this before?)

Suddenly the transmissions were over and I knew it. I was hungry. Very hungry. I ate everything in the house and went to bed. It was eight in the evening, not even dark yet. I went to bed and slept straight through for fourteen hours, might still be sleeping if the telephone company hadn't called the next morning to apologize; my service had been off for three days, and they'd just discovered it. A half hour later my very, very, very psychic friend, George, was at the door wanting to know what was going on. He'd been by three times in two days, he said, and couldn't get past this giant winged thing standing guard outside my door. And so on.

For the next several days I avoided *You* and my living room/couch. It didn't seem to make much difference. Information kept pouring in, more personal and to the point, relevant to the human condition I am currently wading in. I was told that, as my memory of *That*, the "other," comes back, I would probably lose some mundane memory, day-to-day stuff. Names, places, and events that were held in this local memory bank but seldom if ever called on anymore, might be forced off the screen. The rest of the universe is in *all-time-now*; history is not kept and recorded in any linear sense as it is in third density. In the rest of the universe you know everything always, but only what is needed to perform in the *now* is accessible. What you need to know, you do know, and it will be available when you need it. It's not necessary to carry all of it around with you all the time.

In primitive times, when our ancestors went on vision quests or exploring for new worlds, they did so without concern for time. They simply had the experience until it was over. I tried explaining that to my wife one night but she'd have no part of it.

175

Meanwhile, in the process of your remembering *That*, you may become confused at the change in memory patterns, your "automatics"—the way you've always done it—may go through some reprogramming. You may get temporarily dumped off between programs, so that nothing is automatic. You may find yourself driving up and down strange streets wondering where you are. Familiar streets will lose their familiarity. You may experience a moment of panic and fear that you do not know where you are, or who. This won't last long and the results will not be tragic; just enough inconvenience for you to notice it and begin to wonder about yourself.

In the meantime, you may need to take more direct aim at what you intend, no matter how trivial, and *pay attention*.

There is a busy intersection near my house that I have used daily for two years to get in and out of my neighborhood—one of my automatics. Two nights ago I left my house to go visit George. To do that, I should have pulled out of my driveway, driven to the corner, and turned *right*. However, out of habit I turned *left* instead, and ended up at that same busy intersection.

Even before I got there I knew something was wrong.

Nothing was familiar. I sat waiting for the light to change and had no idea where I was, where I was going, or how I'd come to be there. I wasn't even sure why I'd left the house in the first place. I looked at all four corners and didn't recognize a thing on any one of them. The light changed and changed again; no one honked or seemed irritated, but cars did begin to pull around me. The street sign in the intersection said Portland Avenue, and I recognized that, but had no idea where I was in relation to it.

Without a clue, I drove straight ahead, crossed Portland and continued on for perhaps a block before I finally realized where I was, and, more importantly, where I was going. I turned around in someone's driveway, went back to the intersection, and turned toward George's house. Driving away, I looked into my rearview mirror and the intersection I'd just left behind seemed to be breaking up the way the signal on a TV channel might break up were you to lose reception, static waves of light and dark shadows. In front of me, everything was clear, detailed, and well defined. I continued on to George's. While your history is being dumped, you may go through periods of feeling "removed" from everything and everyone. You may even feel some sense of isolation or loss. You are just being separated from the history you no longer need, history that doesn't serve your new-found purpose, history that, in the past, may have disempowered you. You are giving it up. During the process, you may feel more than a little confused. Don't worry, this is not the onset of Alzheimer's. You will get over it, and you will like the difference once you get over how genuinely different it is.

And that's it. At least the part I can remember. It's important to note that much of what they told me I still have no words for. The future lay outside of what my current picture of reality could accommodate. I was told that all this information, and much more, had been downloaded into my aura and was now available on demand should I be asked a question. (Ask me something. Anything.) I was told, too, that many of the tools I would need to work with this material had been placed in my neural circuitry before birth—at my own request, I might add. And I was reminded that this is just one racial memory bank; that I am, in fact, the product of at least twenty-two genetically different races, each represented by its own hologram with its own memory bank. And so on.

This next seemed important: The fact that a majority of you believe something, is cause enough for it to manifest. For that reason, it is more important to know *why* you believe something, than the fact that you believe it.

—from the Journal entry, April 24–May 4, 1999

TOGETHER AGAIN

Just when I thought my old belief system was gone forever, and with it, the god of my childhood, everything was brought back in and made somehow relevant.

Then blown away again.

More in keeping with my own religious upbringing, but no less bizarre, was this next assault on whatever old paradigms I still had hanging around. This is an absolutely true story, but not one I expected my editor to ever let in. In it, Spirit seems determined to expose my own transformation, and does so in a public way. This is very personal and has to do with the pervasive nature of the Divine Spirit, in whatever costume *he* or *she* may choose to wear.

I can't remember who it was that said if you encounter no gods along the path, that's because there are no gods inside of you. Or words to that effect. Put another way: God lives in you as you. I like that. I really like that. In an abstract sense, I even thought I knew what it meant, until this next sequence of events threatened to push me right over the edge of what I thought I knew, bringing me face-to-face with something wonderful and unnerving. If I seem inordinately flip or casual in my treatment of what goes on here, I beg your indulgence. This is so personal in nature, and odd in its happening, I just don't know any other way to handle it. I hope this works out.

It starts in the middle of my class reunion, but I'm not sure what that has to do with anything. Maybe nothing. Quite frankly, I had pretty much decided not to even attend. I had a new publisher, a new book. I was as busy as I've ever been in my life . . . and enjoying it. And besides, each time I go to one of these things I come away suffering some sort of viral syndrome: too much sentiment, too much nostalgia, too much of a good time gone by, all that. However, whether by magic or synchronicity, at the last minute my table seemed to clear, and I ended up going.

Like anyone not actually born yesterday, I grew up at a time in which the world, my town, and my neighborhood were safer than they would ever be again; and as prosperous. (I'm not sure if "safe" means "better," but there it is.) Granted, some of us would go on to make more money and live in nicer homes than our parents, but our lives would never again be as rich. And that's all I'm going to say about that because this is not about that, nor is it about the reunion. The reunion was simply a forum, an opportunity for Spirit to dress up and reveal herself in yet another amazing way.

So we'll skip the caricature descriptions of how my classmates look now, ravaged by time and the details of their lives. Let's just say that everyone looked exactly the way I remembered them: thin, tanned, with all their hair and all their teeth; no one knew where they were going exactly, but they knew they were going all the way. Some had married and spent their entire lives with their high school sweethearts. Some had had their lives razed to the ground and rebuilt, more than once.

On this night, however, everyone had either dealt with their "issues" or left them at home. On the whole, they had survived a lot of heartbreak and arrived at some resolute place in their lives; and maybe, just maybe, that had something to do with what took place. Hearts were open. The collective heart of compassion was open and raw and available. My own heart wide open, I walked right in.

This was in Tulsa, at the Doubletree Hotel in a huge banquet room. We were a large class; over 500 people turned out. We had dinner. The class president welcomed us all back. A disc jockey was playing music from the fifties and sixties, people were dancing, moving around renewing old friendships. This was a sober event, I might add. By that I mean, other than a little wine at dinner, no one was drinking. I was talking to someone, I don't remember who, when someone called *her* name and suddenly there "she" was right in front of me. The most gorgeous female thing in the world. At first I didn't recognize her. "Were you looking for me?" she asked.

"I don't think so," I said.

"Are you sure you're not looking for me?" she asked again.

There was a look in her eye. And I seemed to remember something; more accurately, something seemed to be remembering me. I felt like I was being thought. Or dreamed. Or newly invented on the spot. Her eyes and face were articulate with light. This next came over me in an instant.

Growing up in Tulsa, I lived down the street and around the corner from a young man who was already playing some serious jazz piano around town. He would eventually own the only night-club in our community dedicated solely to jazz. In the era of Elvis Presley and Jerry Lee Lewis, it took some courage on his part. Or maybe it just took a different sensibility. I don't know. He and I were never social, as he was a few years older and we moved in different circles. I was into kid stuff: football, basketball, all that; but I used to greet him as he walked by our house on his way to I don't know where. He was a studious-looking young man, quiet and shy. Seeing him, I would call out his name and say, *"Hello!,"* and he would just nod and smile, without looking in my direction or saying a word.

Whether it was his influence or some peculiarity of my own, I grew up preferring to listen to jazz myself. I even had fantasies of playing the piano someday, of having my own trio and touring the country. However, the thing that made him such a singular event in my life was not his piano playing or his appearance or odd manner, but his wife. His wife. She was my age and she was a quiet nice-looking girl, an accomplished jazz vocalist herself. We went to school together for three years but never spoke. And of course we never dated. Nevertheless, she was the girl I singled out to be of special interest to me. Being my special interest required nothing on her part, it simply meant that she was on my mind night and day, and if I'd had any idea where she lived she would have been under constant surveillance. On my part, it meant that I suffered total disintegration when I passed her in the hall or heard her name. Even then it was her *energy*, her numinous presence, that I was drawn to, without knowing what that meant or what the implications. I had no idea who she really was.

And I suffered in silence.

No one knew.

This was no temporary condition either.

After we got out of school, she began singing regularly at the nightclub she and her husband owned. Night after night, I sat in the shadows and listened to her sing and him play. For reasons too complex and awkward to talk about then or now, I wanted to be him. It was a fantasy that did not soon go away. But not one I had thought about for years. Then someone called her name at the reunion and suddenly there she was in front of me, so close I could touch her body, her face.

"Don't you recognize me?" she said, smiling. "You've been asking for me for days and weeks."

And suddenly I did. I did recognize her.

But I recognized her as someone else, someone who had only recently come forward in my life. Perhaps for the first time I knew who she was, who she really was and had always been. But in that setting, that situation, the recognition was more disturbing than comforting. I mean, we're not talking high school fantasies, phantom lovers, none of that. We're talking goddess stuff here, expressions of the Divine Mother, the Beloved. I have never felt such overwhelming love and compassion in my life as wave after wave of ecstasy washed over me. In the instant that I recognized her it was all I could do to keep from erupting into tears of absolute joy. There She was.

And then She was gone.

I had to ask if that was really her. Someone standing beside me said, really who? and laughed at whatever it was they saw on my face. Apparently no one had noticed anything out of the ordinary. They had not seen who I was talking to or overheard any of our exchange. But when they were reading off the list of classmates now deceased, they called her name.

I was stunned, stoned, near to tears, barely capable of speech. I wondered if perhaps I might be losing my mind. Not a good time or place for it, I thought. But before I could come to any sort of conclusion, a familiar voice called to me over my shoulder.

"Why are you looking over there?" she said. "I'm over here now." And I spun around to see a familiar classmate, a girl I knew and had been speaking to only moments before. Except that her eyes and her voice were now those of the Divine Mother. Before I could respond, her voice changed and the light went out of her eyes.

"Behind you," said that same familiar voice, and I spun around to see yet another classmate, but again with the eyes and voice of the Beloved.

I was crying a little.

And laughing a little.

Doing both at the same time, I was afraid to speak, afraid to load my feelings into words in case they wouldn't hold.

"Are you all right?" said still another class-mate, a man this time, someone I knew, but not well. He was smiling. I looked into his eyes and was utterly amazed. They were Her eyes. The Divine Mother was leaping from one person to another, and I was losing my mind. "Are you all right?" he said again, still smiling, as though at some private joke only he and I were in on.

"No, I'm *not* all right," I said. "I've never *been* all right." And then, "Do you know who you are?"

He laughed. "I'm whoever you want me to be," he said. "I'm You. I'm Her. All of it. Everyone." Then he took me by the arm and suggested we go for a walk, get some air. I needed something, but I wasn't convinced air would help. Nevertheless, I followed him down the hall and outside. I'd forgotten it had been raining all day. The rain had stopped an hour or so earlier; now everything was just muggy and wet. The night air had a sobering effect on me, and it must've done something to him. He looked as though he'd come awake in the middle of a dream. Strangely puzzled, he lit a cigarette, said goodnight, and walked off down the street. I don't think I ever saw him again. I was alone.

But not for long.

A young woman—I say "young," but at that point in the evening, I had no idea how old anyone was—walked up to my side and took me by the arm.

"The thoughts you are having are mine," she said in my mind. I looked down at her and once more fell deep into the eyes and face of the Divine. "Reality is formless and beyond appearances," she said, "an emanation of grace." Uh huh, I thought. But what does that *mean*? I was still laughing a little, crying some. Overwhelmed and overjoyed.

But I'd had enough for one evening. I excused myself and went back to my room. I'd either lost my mind completely, or suddenly found my right mind after a long absence. And I desperately needed to be alone with it.

Once in my room, I washed my face and sat down with my journal, thumbing through the last several entries.

For weeks and months now, my own transformation of consciousness had left me exhausted and raw, physically spent. I just wanted some relief, something soft and nurturing for a change. We forget that we do have that right, that we can ask for some slack now and again. I tend to forget, anyway. My journal, however, showed evidence of serious whining having gone on for quite some time, begging God, in her most gentle nature, to pay me a call. But there was something else there as well, a single entry that I do not recall making. I put it there. It was in my handwriting, so I must have. I just didn't recognize or remember it, and it was dated a full three weeks before the night of the reunion.

All the world is an illusion, it said, a game of lights and shadows. But there is only one Source, one Spirit, one Face. To see that Face in anyone you must look past appearances. Let go of any idea you have about who you think God is and who you think you are. In the eyes of God, You and I are One.

That note in my journal was immediately followed by this, also unrecognized and unidentified: To look into the eyes of God, look into the eyes of your neighbor. Open your heart in this moment and look into the eyes of someone sitting near you and honor them by seeing the face of God in them. Indeed, as you can do that you are seeing your own reflection going all the way back to

Source. Through this exchange of vision, you anchor a matrix within your own heart of Divine love, forgiveness, and compassion for all those things that you thought to have been wrong about yourself or wrong about others or even wrong about what you would call evil in the cosmos.

I closed my journal, a feeling of subdued grace all around me. Then I stretched across the bed with my clothes on, and fell into a deep and dreamless sleep for the first time in days.

At breakfast the next morning everyone was friendly and cordial. No one seemed to recall anything out of the ordinary, or, if they did, they weren't talking about it. Everyone had had a thoroughly good time. And I was of two minds about the events of the night before. I felt wonderfully refreshed and invigorated on the one hand. At the same time, I was inclined to write the evening off as a temporary aberration having to do with the circumstance of the moment. If not for what happened three days later, I probably would have eventually been able to dismiss the entire episode. Here's what happened:

I stayed on in Tulsa for a few more days, working some, but mostly integrating what had just taken place; indeed, was still taking place. The world continued to turn on its axis, the Sun rose in the East, set in the West, all the usual. On the afternoon of the third day out from the reunion, waiting for the cross-town bus at the corner of Eleventh and Harvard, hot, tired, leaning against the shelter, I saw Christ.

It was a crystallizing moment.

Of course, I can only *describe* what took place, not *explain* it; not in any defining way. It's certainly not something that can be readily proved. My hope is that all this at least goes to the weight of the evidence, even as it begs believability. And as I write about these things, I admit to feeling less foolish than I do childlike, overcome with enthusiasm and joy.

It was a simple, clear vision. An old man stood at the curb opposite me, looking thoughtful, pensive, searching the busy street for I don't know what; a break in the traffic perhaps. He looked like a boiled soup bone, wearing a greatcoat and narrow-brimmed cloth hat. He suddenly lowered his head, as if his neck had broken, and saw something that delighted him. He bent down and carefully reached between his feet to pick up whatever it was. He held it up to his face, and smiled. Then with a wave of his hand tossed it into the air. I couldn't see a thing; it was either too delicate, too small, or visible only to him. But the gesture caused him to fall off the curb just as the bus pulled up. He stumbled through the intersection toward me and fell to the pavement at my feet. It was strangely quiet in the street. No cabbies or truck drivers. No honking. No one yelling at us to get out of the way. The bus driver waited patiently for the next thing to happen. From his knees, the palms of his hands scraped and bleeding, an open wound on his forehead, the old man struggled to get up. My response was not immediate. There was a moment of reticence, of unworthiness, and then I bent down to help him. Looking up, he caught my eye for just a moment. It was a moment I have yet to recover from, as if the meaning of a dream were suddenly revealed.

I helped him to his feet, amazed at how light he was. I remember thinking his bones must have been filled with air, or light. I got him to the curb and standing shakily. I put his hat back on his head, wondering, how do you tell Christ that he is Christ. Then I helped him onto the bus where the driver was waiting, smiling, and suddenly he, the bus driver, was Christ, too. The lady in the seat behind the bus driver made room for the old man and suddenly she was Christ. I looked around, the bus was full and Christ was in every seat. Christ was everywhere. I was Christ. I jumped down off the bus and motioned to Christ to drive on, don't wait for me . . . yes, I am going your way, but I'll catch the next one.

I sat down on the bench beneath the shelter, took out my handkerchief and wiped sweat from my eyes. When I looked up again the bus was gone, traffic had resumed, and a fat black lady had joined me on the bench. Christ again, I wondered?

"Are you all right?" she asked.

"Yes," I said. "But I don't know how to tell you about it." I was having a moment that was having everything.

In that moment, I was told that as you remember who God is, you remember who you are; and each spark of memory sends a signal to all minds everywhere, a ripple effect touching every living creature in the deepest chamber of its heart.

Weeks later, reading from my journal and recalling the events recorded above, I continued to have that same moment again and again, enough to spark an incredible surge of enthusiasm and joy. I felt like I might burst open. Which I did, sort of. I mean, I felt wonderfully foolish, unable to stop myself from laughing and crying out loud with only myself to witness, jumping around the room with my hands in the air. If I could fly, I would have. If I could speak in tongues, I would have. HolyMotherofGodAlmightyJesus, I cried. I was a snotty mess, I cried so hard. And I howled like a dog in the moonlight.

Now, I don't know what all this has to do with the ascension that seems to be going on everywhere, how much of it is part of my own "remembering," but it doesn't matter that I don't know. Because it is a complete experience; it is emotional and spiritual and physical; it is passionate; it is fearless and without boundaries. Your own awakening may be private and invisible to all else around you, but it is a total celebration.

—from the Journal, September/October, 1999

Brain Surgery II

This dialogue—arguably a monologue—has gone on for three years now, with little or no interruption, and with no sign of letting up. Actually, most of the information on these pages came quickly, suddenly, within a brief span of time over three years ago. The writing of it, however, has been painfully slow. The reason being that the original communication was holographic in nature. By that I mean, the entire picture, every blueprint, every detail, every event, all of it, came instantly; so much so, that I went into tilt, overload, unable to cognize more than a few, limited segments at a time. I have since been made to remember, *live through*, and integrate each bit of information before I could find words for it. My spirit has always known where we were going. My soul, indeed, my ego had to grow into it gradually, step by step, one transforming event after another. It's a slow and tedious process, but necessary. I cannot write any faster than I can integrate.

By now it is clear to me that no matter the form or disguise of the messenger, some extension of God/the Creator is talking to me. Directly, personally, without doubt. The God within is responding to my need for answers in direct proportion to my ability to comprehend, and by whatever means I can be made to listen—the words of a song, a line from a movie, a passage from a book, a conversation overheard, more often in dreams and meditations, and not the least, in response to inquiries from friends familiar with what is going on with me. I am being informed by every conceivable and inconceivable means. Even as a question is being asked, I *know* the answer in some *feeling* part of myself; then I answer in words and thoughts even I have not heard before, with greater clarity than I knowingly possess, on a range of topics not previously considered.

Once you get past appearances, we do indeed create every single aspect of our environment, projecting an energy field that draws to us the things and people we need to inhabit our reality, and then learn from it.

And there is no limit to where and how far we are able to project that energy field—other dimensions, other universes, other aspects of our own souls, no limits. What makes it interesting is the way in which the brain interprets some of our projections. This goes to my belief that the brain is a reduction valve, a filter. Its function is to reduce the universe to something manageable, something recognizable, and then assign meaning to what it recognizes. When confronted by something absolutely new and foreign, something beyond its programmed limits, it searches its data files for a match. Not finding one, it locates the closest match and identifies it as that. When confronted by a living entity from some other world or dimension, it may identify that as a spacecraft, even a spacecraft resembling a hotel lobby—the Hilton?—and so on. Who is to say that the brain, when confronted by its own soul pattern, might not identify that as a giant mandala; and, further, recognize the workings of the soul as being onboard some mothership of inner space? Who's to say? I mean, is it possible for the brain to know itself, the soul to really search itself? Given our equipment, how can we know?

So, what does that say about my "on board" experiences? Does that make them less real, less actual, less? Not at all. Instead, they have served to break my death-grip on this third dimensional reality that seems so real at times, but is, in fact, no more so than any number of realities in which I am currently participating. In truth, this mundane reality is not even primary; it just happens to be the one I am currently cleaning up and making habitable for the next event. In substance, it is only a shadow world, a colorless and imperfect reflection of my onboard reality. This is just the workplace; onboard is where I live.

And the onboard experiences do go on. Two nights ago I was driving back from Arkansas after visiting with an aunt recovering from brain surgery. It was late. It was cold. I was running a fever. So I decided to take a motel room in Tulsa and just sweat it out overnight.

Actually "fever" is not quite accurate. The highway coming into Tulsa was under construction and I couldn't focus on the road signs or retain what they said. I stopped in an all night grocery and spent half an hour wandering around trying to remember what I'd come for. I don't drink and I haven't done drugs for twenty years, but that's sort of what it felt like. I felt fine, but not well connected. And the clerk must have seen something in my eye, because she followed me down the aisle to ask if I was all right.

In the instant that it took me to do a quick inventory to see if indeed I was all right, I recalled a dream I'd had two nights earlier, a dream in which the Brothers had taken me somewhere in consciousness and sectioned my brain off into four quadrants. One of the quadrants seemed to be on fire, and the Brothers were busy trying to contain the fire and bring all four quadrants into balance. I woke up thinking I really needed to write the dream down but then forgot about it until that moment. And that's what I was thinking when the clerk asked me if I was all right. The look on her face caused me to wonder if maybe my hair was on fire.

That's when I decided to take a motel.

I had difficulty signing the register and felt awkward talking to the motel clerk. I suspect that he suspected that I was drunk or stoned or both. By the time I got into my room and into bed I was cold to the bone and had a crippling headache. Sometime in the night it happened.

I woke up onboard again, this time in a large round room with a domed ceiling and lit by a soft blue light. I seemed to be alone. Actually I seemed to be hiding in a corner of the room observing . . . myself; me on an operating table covered head to toe with a white sheet, in the middle of an observatory. Under the sheet, I wondered if, perhaps, I was dead. In bed in my motel room, I wondered the same thing. It was not a concern, just a curiosity.

As the sheet was pulled down away from my face, the ceiling appeared to roll back as well, revealing the night sky. I watched as an entire galaxy swirled into focus, filling the skylight. Then that galaxy began to shrink in size, but not in detail, as though being seen through a retractable lens, making room for a second complete galaxy. This was repeated again and again until there were seven galaxies lined up all in a row in the sky above me. These are the seven controlling galaxies in the local universe, I was told.

The seventh galaxy seemed to contain the controlling Sun, and was under violent storm clouds. The Brothers were preparing to blow the clouds away (and by "blow" I mean "explode"). I knew the *me* on the table would be affected. I wondered, apprehensively, what effect it would have on me, the observer. My awareness seemed to be in three places at once: on the table, in the shadows watching me on the table, and watching me watch all this. From my bed in my hotel room, I actually flinched in anticipation.

In an explosion of white light, the body on the table appeared to have been struck with a bolt of lightning that lit up the sky in all directions and caused the body to lift a full foot off the table. It so jarred me that I woke up in my hotel room thinking that lightning had struck the electrical outlet at the head of the bed. I thought I smelled burnt wiring. But when I sat up, there was nothing. I went to the window, the night was calm and clear. And my fever was gone.

I went back to bed. But the night was not over.

Sometime before dawn I was visited by another dream-thing, one that keeps coming back every so often, and has for nearly thirty years. I refer to this as my "Einstein dream," but not until this very minute did I realize how relevant and similar it is to things already going on in this book.

Dreams have always played an integral part in my changing consciousness, none more so than the recurring kind. Even before the piano dream was my Einstein dream, a dream so significant and unsettling that it caused me to change my name, my occupation, my date of birth, and eventually brought about the end of my first marriage. My wife was beautiful, sweet, generous, and wrong about me. She thought I had ambition, that I was going somewhere. What she didn't realize was that I'd already been somewhere; as for ambition, it's the universe or nothing for me.

The details of my Einstein dream are peculiar, to say the least, but not that involved: I seem to be on an elevated stage, completely naked, in front of a gallery of childlike beings whose faces I cannot see—friendly, eager for me to do well, but not visible. (Does this sound familiar, not unlike the event that opened this book? Except that this dream first occurred thirty years ago.) I am joined on stage by this Being of brilliant white-light who seems to also be naked, and right in my face. Together we begin to shadow dance, tracking one another's moves identically. I am a little uncomfortable by the proximity, the closeness. But I can't *not* join in. And just when I am about ready to bolt and run, this light being leans forward and puts his or her forehead against mine, and then into mine, and then steps full bodied into me, and suddenly I am dancing, taking leave, taking the lead in a step I have never done. I feel expansive and liberated, wonderfully and entirely alone out there. And then I wake up.

Always, I wake up right there.

I've had this dream a dozen times over the years, and I always wake up in the same place. Initially, my first thought on waking up was that the light being I had been dancing with was, in fact, Albert Einstein. My second thought was that, Albert Einstein is dead. My next thought was to dismiss the first two. Thirty years later, my thinking has changed, but the details of the dream have not. And each recurrence seems to trigger a flood of new insight and information that can sometimes continue for days.

That first dream led me to want to know more about Albert Einstein and his views on quantum physics—neither of which had I had any prior interest in. Interest in Einstein led me to being curious about the Rosicrucians (he was one, as was Ben Franklin, Copernicus, Galileo, Francis Bacon, Thomas Jefferson, and so on). I became interested in all things mystical: astrology, astronomy, ancient history, *pre*-history, mythology, genetics, alchemy, meditation, all that. None of this was in my degree path. Eventually my interests swerved so sharply from where my wife thought we were going that I couldn't deny it any longer. I became a sort of closet mystic. And how do you put that on a resume? What sort of job do you apply for? Thirty years later, I still don't know the answer to that one.

My wife decided that the transformation of consciousness was too risky a business, uninsurable at best. Our interests and awareness went different directions and so did we. Perhaps the most difficult thing I ever had to do in my life was leave my wife and daughter, and not be able to give a good explanation for it. I'm not sure there is one. But I could not have gotten *here* from *there*. And I genuinely like where I am right now, more so than at any previous time.

Thirty years later, and for the first time in at least four years, I woke up in the middle of my Einstein dream again. This time, in a motel room in Tulsa.

GOD IS AN OUTLAW

The next day I slept in, and checked out of the motel late. Spent the better part of the morning talking to myself as though I were someone else (my father in this case) and taking notes.

My earthly father was gone before I was through with him. I have some wonderful memories of him, mostly invented, but real nonetheless. Truth is, I can barely remember what his voice sounded like. And I can't remember him ever saying anything to me of consequence. If he did, and if I remembered it, I'm sure it would go something like this:

You *are* the universe, fool. Your universe is your way of relating to who and what you are. If your vision is short and narrow then your universe will be short and narrow. The universe is the sum of your vision. The center of the universe is wherever you happen to be. Every single thing in the universe is an extension of everything else, a continuum. It's *all* God. And it's all in perfect order. Random doesn't exist in the universe. It is just not possible for disorder to exist in a universe that is ultimately unbroken and whole. The same is true of consciousness. I mean, if a single element of the universe were totally unconscious, the whole universe would be unconscious and random. Any separation of consciousness and matter is an illusion. They are the same thing. Consciousness is simply a more subtle form of matter. Every rock, toad, star, comet, bridge, and automobile has consciousness. The entire universe is made from a single fabric, seamless and holographic in nature. And *everything* has consciousness.

And because everything is a function of consciousness you can move in any direction you like, create any possibility, alter the outcome of any event, affect whatever level of harmony or chaos you choose. What appears as chaos is simply a high degree of order.

So learn to trust the chaos. Chaos is God's natural and unfiltered voice; it is Divine order. And it always accompanies change.

For too long you have played games you do not care about, by rules you do not believe in. If you have been following the rules, and find yourself being angry, negative, resentful, and judgmental, *stop* following the rules for awhile. Stop living by laws and codes of behavior laid down in the dark ages by the god-realm of the fourth dimension. The Creator didn't make the rules you follow. The Creator doesn't *make* you do anything. Life is dynamic creation in action. Experience your own rightness of feeling. Claim your own reality, your own divinity. Stop looking outside yourself for answers. But don't let the negative side of your ego, the martyr, the self-pitying dark side of your self take over. There is joy in risking, in making new, in going beyond the rules. (If the dream is big enough, even the facts don't count.) In the end the choice is always yours, but there are no wrong choices. Each choice has its consequence, but the only moral criterion is love—for oneself, one's neighbor, one's enemy, one's life.

God/the Creator wants you to be happy and secure in a deep spiritual sense. But it is madness to think that God is represented by the events or contents of your ego/material life. Stop measuring your relationship with God by whether or not you like your job, enjoy your life, or are getting laid properly. God is not a romantic. She doesn't care what you do or who you are doing it to.

The path of the Spirit is not the path of human matter; it is a deviation from the norm, from the rational, from anything egoistically coherent. To have an intimate relationship with the living Spirit you must be willing to enter into chaos and recognize the clarity in it, the divine order that transcends human order; learn to live in and with a mystery that cannot be explained in human terms, and be at home in the uncertainty. Stay balanced in there. Stay conscious, fully alive, excited, exciting, curious, and peaceful, all within the same one mystery.

And stop expecting God to behave like a rational human being. God is neither rational nor human.

Nor is God a fortune teller, a judge, or an accountant. Living by grace that transcends any law or rule of decorum, God is an *outlaw*. And the universe is exactly what you think it is. (What you think, is.) Any set idea you may have about the organization and structure of the universe helps to mold and create that structure. If you don't like the universal hologram you are presently in, change your way of thinking. No single hologram, no one reality, nor any single cause-and-effect relationship can ever explain the infinite. Know this: If you can name it, define it, or describe it, that's probably not it.

APPENDIX I: A MEDITATION

The ego regards any change as threatening, whether that change be in the personal self or the world you have created around you. Faced with change, the ego solicits help from the intellect, and together they drag your mind up and down countless avenues of thought and thinking, distractions designed to put the ego back in control. The heart, listening to the mind and finding no answers, no safe haven, becomes fearful and eventually closes.

The key to personal transformation is to keep your mind still and your heart open. Most of you are in the habit of doing just the opposite. Your sense of separation, anger, and fear comes from the mind's incessant chatter, depending on the ego/intellect to rationalize, read, or otherwise think your way through a problem. When the mind fails, the heart shrinks back in fear. It is your own mind that causes your heart to close, and when the heart is closed, the Universe cannot nourish you.

In these times of rapid transformation, learn to quiet the mind by breathing, by meditating on the breath and going "inside" your own stream, your own current.

Prana is breath endowed with consciousness; it is the life force and it flows in a constant stream from the Source into and through your entire being. Learn to breathe prana in through the top of your head and up from your perineum at the same time, from above and below in a circular, counter-rotating motion (If you're not sure how to do this, your intention and a good faith effort is enough).

Inside you is a current of light about two inches in diameter that runs through the center of your being, up and down your spine, extending slightly above your head and below your feet. This is the prana tube. Learn to breathe through it. Breathe prana *in* from above and below at the same time, allowing it to meet in the pineal gland in the center of your head—slightly above and between the eyes and the ears.

On the *out*breath, hold your consciousness in the pineal gland while you pulse the energy both directions at once, up the tube, out through the top of the head and into the sky; at the same time you are pulsing it down the tube, out, and into the earth below, always concentrating in the center of your head.

I usually begin my meditations with a prayer of sorts, something like this:

"Mother/Father/God, make me the medium and the means for unconditional love. Teach me to live with attention, cultivate compassion, and serve without concern for the outcome; and, in so doing, realize the purpose for which I am created."

Now, in a single connected motion, without pausing at either end of the breath, breathe *in* from above and below, counter-rotating to meet while you push your breath *out* the tube in both directions at once, into the earth and into the sky. Do this at least seven times, or until you are firmly centered in the pineal gland. (See "Activating Your Merkabah," next page.)

On the next breath, on the *out*breath, and still centered in the pineal gland, let the prana radiate out into a sphere large enough to encompass the heart. Do this three times. Then meditate there for a few minutes, breathing in from above and below, holding your consciousness in the pineal gland, breathing out into a sphere that encompasses the heart.

As the heart begins to relax and feel safe, on the next *out*breath, make the sphere large enough to include your entire body. On the next *out*-breath, expand the sphere to include your home; on the next, include your neighborhood, then your city, the planet, the galaxy, the Universe, all dimensions. All the time, sitting quietly and following the breath, concentrating on the breath, breathing and watching your breathing.

If you have thoughts—and you will—don't follow them. Don't resist them, but don't follow them. Just let them come and go without relish, watching each thought with equal interest and no comment.

When you refuse to follow this or that thought or feeling, and simply allow each to rise and fall of its own accord without opinion, judgment, or reaction, the mind slowly ceases its chattering. A deep quiet emerges. Thought ceases, and with it, the fears of the mind.

Once the ego self is empty and the mind is peaceful, the heart will open of its own accord. It opens to the deep Self, the *feeling nature* of the deep Self—not the look of it, certainly not some vague thought or idea of it—but the overwhelming sense of unity in God that comes from *knowing* the deep Self. The heart experiences this sense of unity as a deep and expansive love for creation in all its separate details.

The emptying of self and the repairing of the world with love are two sides of the same spiritual practice. We are not seeking to escape the world, we are seeking to transform it. In order to transform the world, it is necessary to transform your self.

I close my meditations with something like this:

"Mother/Father/God, give me, give each of us, that which we are in most need of; give us clarity of purpose, right intent, and the courage to stay/be in integrity at all times."

Come back into your body slowly, bringing as much of this consciousness with you as you can.

Activating Your Merkabah

Merkabah is simply the term for your spirit-body surrounded by counter-rotating fields of light. The merkabah itself consists of two interlocked star tetrahedrons, counter-rotating in a single space and at such a speed they may appear as spheres of light.

If you are working with your *merkabah/light-body,* after the initial seven breaths of the meditation, and centering in the pineal gland, instead of radiating out into spheres, activate your merkabah. This is done by spinning the lower merkabah counterclockwise, from right to left, while spinning the upper merkabah clockwise, from left to right, and using "om-merkabah" as a mantra, chanting "om" on the *in*breath while counter-rotating the energy from above and below, and chanting "merkabah" on the *out*breath while visualizing the merkabah itself.

Use of the merkabah activates synchronicity—what you need, the Universe will put immediately in your path—and it makes the ascension process possible by disengaging you from the cycle of karma and reincarnation.

Again, if you're not sure how to do this, your *intention* and a good faith effort will go a long way.

When you don't have time to meditate

Remember, there is a constant flow of Divine energy that enters through the top of the head as a thin current of light running through the center of our being, and located in the spine. It is lovingly impersonal as it enters the head; however, it becomes more dense and personal as it sinks deeper into the body. Should life become too dense and too personal, or should the stress of any of your lower chakras become temporarily unmanageable, remember that same current runs *up* the spine and out through the top of the head, connecting us with the *Source*. Should we forget our own divine origins, or should we desire to be free of the turbulence of the third or fourth dimensions, even while working in them, *stay in the current*. Abandon all belief systems, look up, literally through the top of the head, and focus on, and *breath in*, That—the God Within.

APPENDIX II: A BRIEF GLOSSARY

Note: The following definitions are not intended to exclude or minimize any understandings you may already have; they are by no means conclusive, and should be considered in their context.

Chakra

The word chakra literally means circle or wheel. The chakras are energy or psychic nerve centers in the body, points where soul and body connect and interpenetrate each other; storing information, memories, and emotions encoded as energy, the chakras work like frequency transformers, connecting your energy bodies by stepping the energy up or down between them as necessary.

Fifth dimension

Operating outside of linear time and space, this is the dimension of instant manifestation (fishes and loaves, all that). What one thinks, one becomes. The first movement of particles into form occurs here—this is the dimension of Christ-consciousness.

Fourth dimension

The patterns of form, time, and space that govern the entire third dimension are created here; it is our thoughts and dreams generated in the fourth dimension that hold the third dimension in form/place. This is the god-realm, the dimension where belief systems are built and maintained.

Great White Brotherhood

A race of perfected beings who have chosen to help the human species along the evolutionary path.

Karma

Put simply, this is the law of cause and effect. What one does (or causes) carries with it the responsibility and rewards of its effect; and it is the *intention* of the action that causes a karmic effect to arise. Karma is made complex by the fact that it operates over many lifetimes—because conditions must be appropriate for karma to ripen, the *cause* and its resulting *effect* may be separated by many lifetimes.

Kundalini

This is the evolutionary energy in man, the life force that sits like a smoldering coal at the base of the spine (the coccyx). The kundalini is the spiritual force that lies dormant in every human being, and once awakened, it has the potential to shoot up the spine like a stream of liquid light, activating one chakra after another, entering the brain and the nervous system, causing an emotional and physical cleansing, and enabling the body to reconstruct itself. Along the way, it can cause all manner of imbalances to occur. Mood swings and physiological and psychic side effects continue until one is finally able to stabilize at a higher level of consciousness and find expression in the form of spiritual insight, mystical vision, psychic powers, and ultimately, enlightenment.

Mechanical causation
This has to do with that aspect of cause and effect which is confined to the third and, to some extent, the fourth dimensions—which are measured and defined by linear time and space. In mechanical causation cause must always precede its effect.

One Mind
The undifferentiated Mind of God; nothing and no one is separate from anything else.

Resonant causation
Responding simply to the vibration of one's consciousness, resonant causation makes it possible to generate an effect without prior cause. Knowing who you are and emanating who you are cause the evolution of everything in your environment to accelerate. Operating without the limitations of space and time, resonant causation is of quantum proportions, bound only by your ability to imagine and know.

Sixth-dimensional physics
This is Sacred geometry—the geometry of pre-form, on which form itself depends, manifesting first as geometric light.

INDEX